A PASSION FOR THIS EARTH

INSPIRED BY DAVID SUZUKI

WRITERS, SCIENTISTS,

AND ACTIVISTS EXPLORE OUR

RELATIONSHIP WITH

NATURE AND THE ENVIRONMENT

FOREWORD BY **BILL McKIBBEN**

EDITED BY **MICHELLE BENJAMIN**

— A —

PASSION

FOR THIS

EARTH

David Suzuki Foundation

GREYSTONE BOOKS

Douglas & McIntyre Publishing Group

VANCOUVER/TORONTO/BERKELEY

Greystone Books
A division of Douglas & McIntyre Ltd.
2323 Quebec Street, Suite 201
Vancouver, British Columbia
Canada. V5T 4S7
www.greystonebooks.com

David Suzuki Foundation
2211 West 4th Avenue, Suite 219
Vancouver, British Columbia V6K 4S2

Library and Archives Canada Cataloguing in Publication
A passion for this earth / foreword by Bill McKibben ; edited by Michelle Benjamin.

Co-published by the David Suzuki Foundation.
Includes bibliographical references.

ISBN 978-1-55365-375-2

1. Human ecology. 2. Environmental protection.
3. Nature—Psychological aspects. 4. Environmentalism.
5. Environmental policy. I. Benjamin, Michelle II. David Suzuki Foundation

QH75.P375 2008   333.7   C2008-900377-2

Editing by Nancy Flight
Cover design by Jessica Sullivan
Text design by Naomi MacDougall
Cover photograph © Momatiuk-Eastcott/CORBIS
Printed and bound in Canada by Friesens
Printed on acid-free paper that is forest friendly (100% post-consumer recycled paper) and has been processed chlorine free.
Distributed in the U.S. by Publishers Group West

We gratefully acknowledge the financial support of the Canada Council for the Arts, the British Columbia Arts Council, the Province of British Columbia through the Book Publishing Tax Credit, and the Government of Canada through the Book Publishing Industry Development Program (BPIDP) for our publishing activities.

CONTENTS

TRAVELS WITH DAVID SUZUKI

FOREWORD

THERE'S REALLY NO ONE ON EARTH QUITE LIKE
David Suzuki, and this volume illustrates why.

In his early life, Suzuki was perhaps Canada's finest
bench scientist—John Lucchesi's recollections set the
scene and make his lab sound wonderfully alive. More
than a lifetime's work.

But that wasn't enough. Life on a microscale was fas-
cinating to him, but so was life macroversion. Trees and
whales and lichen and birds—soon he had translated his
passion for the world around him into the planet's most
popular nature program. Those who think this is an easy
task should survey the field: endless British-accented documentaries drying up the natural human love for wild
things. Instead, Suzuki turned people on, turned them
on to the delights that so many describe in these pages.
He became the terrestrial version of Jacques Cousteau,
translator of all that was wonderful into the vernacular

of a culture that had turned away from the natural. More than a lifetime's work.

But that wasn't enough either. It's always hard to say where the thirst for political action comes from, the thirst for justice. Perhaps it was Suzuki's early days in an internment camp during World War II; certainly it was the sight of all that he cared about being quickly blender-ized by the onslaught of "progress." And so he rose up and fought. Fought eloquently, with his voice and his personal witness. Fought diligently, with his foundation and his reporting. Fought fairly, cleanly, nobly.

Does it matter? It's mattered enormously along Can-ada's Pacific coast and in dozens of other specific places. It's too early to know if it's mattered enough on the great question of the day, climate change, but as several of these essays make clear, his passion and his relentless intelligence have surely helped turn the tide.

The variety of essays in this book is the surest testa-ment to Suzuki's life. There are very few other people for whom it would make perfect sense to write about global warming policy, as Ross Gelbspan does, and about media reform and its impact on the Earth, as Doug Moss does, and about the magnificent *Carapa* tree, as Adrian Forsyth does. Most of us pick one area and dig in.

But the central truth of ecology, the great emergent science of our time, is that everything is connected. And in the cultural ecology, Suzuki is one of those connectors, a crucial hub in the network that Paul Hawken describes as spreading across the Earth. Connecting biology and policy and economics and art, never afraid of the activism that charges those connections, Suzuki has become an organizing principle. The world is not entirely lucky at the moment—in fact, it looks as if we're entering a period of enormous stress, whose outcome is by no means assured. But we're lucky indeed to have a man like David Suzuki and to be able to honor him with our words.

Bill McKibben

FALLING

in LOVE *with*

the WILD

The way we see the world

shapes the way we treat it. If a mountain

is a deity, not a pile of ore; if a river is one

of the veins of the land, not potential

irrigation water; if a forest is a sacred grove,

not timber; if other species are our biological

kin, not resources; or if the planet is our

mother, not an opportunity—then we

will treat each one with greater respect.

This is the challenge, to look at the world

from a different perspective.

{ DAVID SUZUKI }

SAVED BY THE SEA

David Helvarg

MY SISTER RECENTLY DIED AND THAT GOT ME thinking about our childhood. My best memories of our growing up on New York's Long Island Sound involved water—standing, brackish, and salty.

My friends and I used to play in the swamp behind our school and wade around in the sound's shallows searching the muddy waters with our feet for the primitive armored shapes of horseshoe crabs, which we would lift up by their spiky tails for closer inspection. Early on our boys' culture divided between those of us who defended the rights of horseshoe crabs to be played with and skipped across the water and older "hoods" who liked to imprison them in rock corrals and then smash their shells with heavy stones. After one fight in which by dint of numbers we vanquished a group of "hoods," a gray-haired eel fisherman came over to congratulate us, explaining how sometimes you have to fight for the creatures who can't fight for themselves.

Today there are thousands of grown-up kids defending horseshoe crabs, American eels, and other creatures threatened with extinction. Along the Jersey and Delaware shores, where millions of horseshoe crabs have been harvested for eel bait and the loss of their multitudinous eggs threatens migrating shorebirds, marine activists have won new protections for these animals that were ancient when dinosaurs were the coming thing. Others are defending the endangered American eel, whose Homeric journey from the Sargasso Sea along the Gulf Stream to the headwaters of North America's eastern rivers is now hampered by dams, development, and a global seafood market that includes Asian demand for "glass eels" or baby "elvers," which once sold for as much as ten dollars a pound.

As a result of industrial overfishing, 90 percent of the large predator fish have been eliminated from the world's oceans since 1950, according to the late Ran Myers and Boris Worm of Dalhousie University. This is only one of a cascading series of disasters confronting our living seas. There's the nutrient, chemical, and plastic poisoning of our coastal and deep waters; the construction boom and sprawl destroying the life-giving habitats needed for marine restoration, including salt marshes and other briny places that act as the filters and nurseries of the sea; and a fossil-fuel-driven climate shift that's raising sea levels, melting ice shelves, intensifying hurricanes, bleaching corals, and making the oceans more acidic. I saw what the future may bring as I traveled the smashed and empty streets of New Orleans, the drowned bayou of Louisiana, and the devastated Gulf Coast in the wake of Hurricane Katrina. It reminded me of wars I'd covered only with fewer deaths, far wider destruction, and a million environmental refugees.

When I was eight I wanted to be a navy frogman and fight for dolphins and America. By eleven I was thinking I'd become an oceanographer and was addicted to *Sea Hunt* and Jacques Cousteau on TV. At thirteen I went to my first civil rights demonstration and got swept away by the social movements and moments of my youth.

Then there was that missed opportunity, a life course not taken when I was sixteen and my mother took my sister, Deborah, and me on a road trip to Key West. Driving over the ocean on the old two-lane-highway bridge, looking out at the jade and aquamarine reef line, I felt I'd come home to a place I'd never seen before. We stopped at Pigeon Key, where the University of Miami had converted an old cabin resort into a research station and a storm had broken over the old swimming pool, smashing and filling it with live coral and big jacks and parrot fish. We stayed at the old Key Wester out by the airport and toured the Key West Aquarium full of big jewfish (now called goliath groupers), moray eels, barracuda, sergeant

5

majors, queen angels. As I identified them, my mother turned to my sister and said, "Gee, I guess he doesn't just make all this stuff up."

"I remember that. I was surprised you knew all those fish names," my sister tells me as we sit out on her porch in Brookline, Massachusetts, a week before she passes, the early-winter sun warming our faces, both of us now in our fifties, set in our own ways, comfortable with our common history.

As a young kid, I'd looked up at the stars and gotten pissed off, thinking I'd been born a generation too soon to explore other worlds. But that week in Key West I got hold of a mask and snorkel and got into the water and saw live rocks, and vibrant colors, sea cucumbers and a queen conch, a sea turtle and a small hammerhead gliding through a coral canyon amid shoaling fish and realized there was this whole other alien world right beyond the seawall. Sadly, in the blink of an eye that's been my life, the Keys reef has gone from 90 percent live coral cover to less than 10 percent, devastated by pollution, physical impacts from boats, anchors and people and global warming. One night we went to the Kraals Restaurant, which still had big sea turtles in pens, and my mother had the turtle soup and let me order a vodka, and when I swallowed too much and grimaced she turned to my sister and said, "Does he make a face like that when he smokes pot?" We were both shocked.

I could have run off to sea right then. But there was a war dividing the nation and we had to get back home to

New York, where Martin Luther King soon came to speak at our high school.

"I wonder how we would have turned out differently if not for the sixties," my sister says.

"Maybe you wouldn't have ended up doing all your medical work or being the great mom you are," I suggest. She looks unconvinced.

"Maybe we should just be in the moment," I say.

She gives me an odd look then grins. "Right, that California stuff," but is quiet and relaxed in the sun, pain-free for a time before getting back to worrying about Adam and Ethan, her boys of sixteen and eighteen.

At seventeen I ran off to protest at the Democratic convention in Chicago, where the police rioted and I got my first taste of mace, gas, and blunt force trauma. At eighteen I was busted and beaten for fighting back. When I was twenty-one, a right-wing terrorist group targeted my friends and me on the beach in San Diego (we were organizing protests against Richard Nixon's Republican convention). By the time I was twenty-two, it was pretty clear there wasn't going to be urban guerilla warfare in America, so I went to Belfast as a reporter to see what it looked like.

It looked pretty mean but was personally challenging. It made me better able to understand the axiom that in war, truth is the first casualty. The British–IRA conflict in Ulster also made me realize I had a vocation for writing and reporting. After five months I returned to my flat from the scene of a car bombing and shoot-out only to get word my mother had contracted lung cancer (she was a pack-and-a-half-a-day woman). I sat down by the ruins of the recently bombed Brooke Park Public Library. Someone had a radio on. It was playing Paul Simon's "Mother and Child Reunion." I flew home and helped care for her in the few months before she died. I then moved back to the beach in San Diego, where I built a career as a freelance journalist, while also finding time to bodysurf.

The Pacific Ocean took me back to the salty dreams of my childhood. I started writing stories about navy dolphins, sharks, offshore oil and mining, whatever could keep me connected to the everlasting sea. When my dad died a few years later I was living with a couple of buddies in a brown clapboard cliff house sixty feet above the ocean. To overcome my grief I went off to cover wars in Central America for five years. I went with a good friend, photographer John Hoagland. Between reporting under fire and covering civilian massacres and death squads, we'd go to the beach in El Salvador to recharge. John, a longtime surfer, liked the left break at La Libertad. I dug the long barrels along the Costa del Oro, even if I did spot the occasional bull shark in the surf line. After John and Richard Cross, another good friend who was like a brother, were killed in combat, I returned to the beach in San Diego and got my Private Investigator's license.

Then I moved to the Bay Area, got scuba certified, and met Nancy Ledansky. She was my adventure mate and life's love. We ended up in a duplex looking down on

Richardson Bay in Sausalito. We dove Australia, Mexico, the Caribbean, went to Hawaii and coastal Alaska, hiked Point Reyes National Seashore every other weekend. We got shipwrecked during a storm in Baja before refloating the boat (which was then towed and sunk by the Mexican Navy). Another time she got jealous when I rode a whale shark, which she didn't know was a vegetarian. "It's lucky he didn't mistake you for a veggie burger," she groused.

We broke up, but not cleanly. I moved to DC, away from her and my other love, the sea. Right after I started writing the ocean book I'd always wanted to, she found a lump in her breast. I was with her through the chemo, which was awful but seemed to work. I finished *Blue Frontier* and was on the Deep East Expedition one hundred miles off Nantucket when Al Qaeda hit the twin towers. When I got back to land she told me her cancer was back. I was with her for the last few months, in the hospital and home hospice, where we could watch the waters of the bay flowing in and out with the tide.

After she died at forty-three we had a memorial service on one of her favorite beaches. It was a gusty day, feisty like the gal, with the winds whipping the sand and frothing the cold translucent waves. She used to say I never looked happier than when I was coming out of the water after getting beat up by the waves. But the ocean can also provide solace, give you a sense of being a part of something larger, even when large parts of your own soul have torn away.

9

I moved back to Washington with our cat, not sure what to do next, not sure I wanted there to be a next. I found I had three options. I could return to California and do more PI work for Scott, a lawyer friend and diving buddy, but I'd already done enough of that. I could return to war reporting, as President Bush was then planning a pre-emptive war on Iraq, and that had some appeal, war having once proved an effective antidote to depression. I also started meeting with Ralph Nader, who had read my book and encouraged me to organize the Seaweed Rebellion that I describe in its final chapter. He offered me some support, including free office space amid a rabbit warren of public interest start-ups in a building near Dupont Circle.

After a lot of reflection I decided that while we'll probably always have wars, we may not always have wild fish, living reefs, or protective coastal wetlands. I thought about the work of people I knew or who had inspired me: David Brower, Rachael Carson, Jacques Cousteau, David Suzuki, Ralph. I decided to go with my surviving love. Plus if I went to war I didn't know what I'd do with the cat. So the Poose, who hated getting even her paws wet, brought me back to the sea.

And there were these other factors, of course.

Salt water covers 71 percent of the "Earth's" surface and provides 97 percent of its livable habitat. While the tropical rain forests have been called the lungs of the world, the oceans actually absorb far greater amounts of carbon dioxide. Microscopic phytoplankton in the top layer of the sea acts as a biological pump extracting some 2.5 billion tons of organic carbon out of the atmosphere annually, replacing it with 70 percent of the life-giving oxygen we need to survive. The top two feet of seawater contains as much heat as the entire atmosphere.

Photosynthesis of carbon dioxide by plankton and terrestrial plants was thought to be the basis of all organic life until 1977, when scientists aboard a deep-diving submarine off the Galapagos Islands discovered sulfurous hot water vents eight thousand feet below the surface colonized by giant tube worms, clams, white crabs, and other animals that contain sulfur-burning bacteria, which provide an alternative basis for sustaining life. Now NASA scientists believe similar "chemosynthetic" life-forms may exist around volcanic deep-water ocean vents beneath the icy crust of Jupiter's moon Europa. Like I said before, whole other alien worlds right here on our own ocean planet, strange worlds both awesome and familiar. Our bodies, like the planet, are 71 percent salt water, our blood exactly as salty as the sea (when our ancestors emerged from it). This fact may explain why it's easier to fall asleep to the sound of the ocean. The rhythm of the waves is like our mother's heartbeat. For seven years I'd lived in that cliff house in San Diego that shook when the storm waves rolled in every winter. I never slept better in my life.

And so I followed the rhythm. In December 2002, after talking it over with many seaweed (marine

11

grassroots) activists I'd met and deeply liked, and after being assured I wasn't stepping on anyone's flippers, I established the Blue Frontier Campaign. The idea was to strengthen the ocean constituency and help mobilize a blue movement that could change policy from the bottom up. My sister was also happy I wasn't going back to war.

In the next few years we got a lot done with a staff of two and many interns, friends, and volunteers. We held book events and "Celebrations of the Sea" for over 3,000 people including scientists, fishermen, surfers, divers, members of Congress, and others. We held a three-day conference for 250 activists from 170 organizations, and a smaller mid-Atlantic regional conference at the National Aquarium in Baltimore. We produced the first *Ocean and Coastal Conservation Guide* in print and online, listing some 2,000 "blue" groups and ocean parks. We established a website and a monthly "Blue Notes" ocean policy newsletter, wrote guides for activists, distributed free books and other materials, and produced articles, videos, opinion pieces, and radio reports for a range of national and global media. I spoke to anyone I could and wrote 50 *Ways to Save the Ocean* (with a foreword by Philippe Cousteau and illustrations by "Sherman's Lagoon" cartoonist Jim Toomey) as a way for everyone and anyone who gets something from the ocean, whether it be recreation, transportation, energy, security, protein, or spiritual renewal, to give something back. The number one way is "Go to the Beach," because you're more likely to protect that which you love.

12

The biggest personal setback was that in trying to save the ocean from a concrete-covered swamp—Washington, DC—I had far less water time. And so, recently thinking about the time we're allotted and the need to do what gives us passion and be where we belong, I moved back to California, a place my nephews also like to visit.

And here I am, back in cold water with Captain Jessie Alstatt of the Santa Barbara Channelkeeper. We're off Anacapa Island, California, where the keepers are tending the first-ever open ocean eel grass restoration project, part of the panoply of solutions that could still help turn the tide. The bottom where we drop in is littered with brittle stars. Closer to the eel grass beds are freestanding stalks of giant kelp, senorita and lizard fish, gobies, sand dabs, orange-throat blennys peeking out from abandoned worm tubes, and a big bat ray just hanging out. And because each dive's unique, I get to meet my first sarcastic fringehead, a mottled shovel-mouthed fish that, if it were nine feet instead of nine inches would be the terror of the sea.

Back on board we watch leaping dolphins, sea lions, and diving pelicans feeding on a live bait ball. I am cold, wet, salty, and grinning like a fool. At moments like this, enveloped by the wonder of the everlasting sea, it's hard, despite the best available science, not to be optimistic.

THE QUESTION

—— *Rick Bass* ——

FOR A FEW YEARS AFTER MOVING UP HERE TO THE Yaak Valley of extreme northwestern Montana, I would wake up almost every morning wondering whether I was taking the right course. I had quit my company job as an oil-and-gas geologist, and was easing away from my job as a consultant, and had begun dabbling in fiction, only to get sucked, almost immediately, into activism: trying to help protect these wild places I was falling in love with. Had fallen in love with.

My transition from artistic pacifist to activist came pretty quickly, though certainly not all at once. When I arrived in this sylvan valley, warfare, strife, desperation, and the bitterness of steady defeat were—thank goodness!—the furthest things from my mind. I was young and strong, and everything I saw—everything—was new and wonderful. The Yaak is right on the U.S.–Canada border—indeed, there is a similarly named valley, the Yahk, just across the line, a stone's long throw to British Columbia. I went for long walks through old dark forests, on both sides of the border back then, and hiked to the tops of distant mountains, where I beheld beautiful views. Time seemed to be stopped cold in its tracks, for whenever I blinked, there was something new, something outlandish. My first sighting of a wolverine, first grizzly, first wolf. First princess pine, first kinnikinnick, first moose with summer velvet antlers, first marten, first harlequin duck, first bog orchid, first everything.

And, in the natural order of things, first summer, first autumn, winter, and spring.

It was around that second summer, as I recall, that my mind began to make comparisons—to notice what all was going on around me, and the rate of that change. I had experienced four full seasons, which provided me with a reference point for assessing the destructive environmental practices—namely, the rampant clear-cuts and the plowing of dusty roads deep into the forest—that were proceeding.

That first year, I had noticed no harm, no fouls, because it had all been new and, as such, frozen for me in time.

But it didn't take long. By the second year I had it figured out that those old clear-cuts were still being made anew, elsewhere around the valley, and it didn't take a rocket scientist to figure out there had to be a better way; nor did it take a genius to do the math and look at the valley, or even a map of the valley, and extrapolate from the frenetic activity the arc of what-was-to-come.

I eased into it at first. There weren't a lot of local conservation efforts in the Yaak, per se—what little there was back then was focused more on the majestic narrow rock-and-ice blade of the Cabinet Mountains, just to the south—but I began attending some of the meetings of the Cabinet-minded folks, and some of the Forest Service's public meetings, too, particularly those that concerned the proposed management for grizzly bears and mines and issues relating to the wilderness, or the lack of it.

It was a pretty steep learning curve, and pretty rough country in which to be an environmentalist. The Champion Mill was running at peak capacity, employing about a thousand people (in a town of 2,400), and the mines were blowing and going, too. That was about it for jobs: it was essentially a one-horse company town, subservient to the commodities markets. When the loggers and miners got in my face, I tended to jaw right back at them. I'd probably do it the same way all over again, but that's not how I do it now—or not as much, anyway. These days I'm far more interested in winning than in fighting. I have a deep sense that the clock is running out.

Being a writer, I started to write about these issues, in addition to attending meetings. It seemed inconceivable to me that such amazing country possessed no permanent protection whatsoever—just as there was no significant protection for the Yahk in British Columbia, either—and certainly no discussion of plans for a special co-management strategy in this vital and valuable region. Surely it was simply an oversight. And I thought that once I brought that oversight to the agency's and Congress's attention, there would be but a short time period before a strategy was put in place. It might take a year of pretty hard and focused work, I theorized, or maybe, given government's slowness, even a year and a half. I was more than willing to take that time off from my craft and devote it to the mountains and the valley. A full year seemed like a pretty long time, but so what? Brimming with energy, I had time on my hands, and—or so I believed—time on my side. The fact that there had never been any wilderness designated in the Yaak simply meant to my opportunistic mind that the time had come.

THERE WAS SO much change for me back then, coming in so short a time. Was I right to abandon those new joys of fiction writing and the raw freedom of never knowing what each day would bring—never knowing the turns a story would take and, in fact, following most stories in the opposite direction from where I might ordinarily have expected them to wander—and to instead launch myself—carelessly, recklessly, wantonly, daily—into advocacy on behalf of the last roadless areas in a small wild valley? Back then I never dreamed that strength, energy, endurance, might someday be available in anything less than infinite supply.

It's the wildest and most diverse valley I've ever seen in the lower 48, with grizzlies prowling around in the forests down to elevations as low as 2,000 feet, as well as lynx, wolverines, wolves, sturgeon in the Kootenai River, great gray owls, bull trout, eagles, and on and on. Still, despite this wildness, there is not one single acre of protected wilderness in the million-acre valley.

The question I used to ask myself—every morning—was a simple question, one to which—each morning—I had only to answer yes or no. Should I write about this valley in the real world, in real life—or should I continue on with my new joy, fiction: made-up stories about make-believe lives in make-believe places?

Should I just keep quiet about the damage—the injustices—being done to the Yaak?

This ravaged valley, which has been clear-cut to hell and back—only a tattered archipelago of roadless cores remains intact—might be better off without my voice, in almost every regard save that of my own conscience. The current human community of hermits and government loathers that lives here might be more at ease were the plight of this valley's roadless lands still a secret, just as the present grizzly bear community (which at that point had dwindled rapidly to one remaining breeding-age female; now there are three) might be better off, in the next few years, if I'd just lain low and been quiet. The old ways of road building and clear-cutting are maybe just about gone, or surely soon to be gone, aren't they? (Although only ten or twenty years ago, they were not just about gone.)

It's true that the Yaak has been hacked hard, but maybe that's all over. Wasn't there a chance that without my even having to say anything, or advocate for anything, things would just stay the way they are—which is pretty much the way all of us up here, myself included, want them to stay? That's the question.

I didn't hear many other voices speaking out, either in the community or in the larger, more empowered world, on behalf of the Yaak's roadless cores. So I stepped up my efforts, publishing even more information about this oversight and asking for help. I made my decision, even though I suspected the news of yet another significant place in peril might bring onlookers whose ephemeral visits could occasionally, like a brief rainstorm, compromise the peace of the hermits such as myself and the grizzlies, the wolves. (There aren't many trails in the Yaak, and fewer vistas, in these dense woods; as far as human recreation goes, a beer at the tavern, or a beer at the Dirty Shame, about covers it). Still . . . Tourists?

It's not a beautiful valley, really, to many visitors: it's dark and rainy and snowy and spooky. (This fall, we've had only four days of sunshine out of the last hundred). The locals can be unfriendly, and there are many biting insects and much fog and rain and snow. Unlike most places in the world, this is a great place to live but not much to visit. My worst fear nonetheless is of a wave of yuppie acquisition, the gnawing, consuming contagion of looking at a landscape and thinking, What's in it for me?

And yet: to be quiet about injustice? Either answer seemed a hard one.

TOURISM IS NOT the answer for this ragged place. The group with which I've started volunteering, the Yaak Valley Forest Council, has been working for the last many years to get some small timber sales of dead and dying trees, using existing road systems to access those sales, with those trees set aside for the handful of loggers who still live in the valley, and to give the local small-mill owners first-right-of-refusal on those logs.

This step won't change the world. It won't save that culture. But it will buy time, which is almost the same thing. Nothing lasts forever.

Many of the woods workers are scared to death of me: frightened and angry. They think that the establishment of protected wilderness areas in the last roadless cores that remain would only be the beginning. They believe that the government would then begin evicting them from house and home, devouring the entire community in that fashion, as the old clear-cutters once devoured whole mountains up here.

So I'm caught between two worlds, as I was once caught between fiction and advocacy: working for the last

20

few bands of independent loggers and mill owners, and working, still, as ever, for the little unprotected wilderness that still remains. Moving back and forth, here and there, in the worst combination of both restlessness and weariness. Believing fully that there is still room for both.

What I like about the notion of wilderness designation is that I could stop fighting, year after year, on behalf of roadless areas. I could go back to my other life—if it still waits there for me. I don't think backpackers would flock to the Yaak. There are few trails and fewer vistas. It's not like the rest of the West. It's a swamp—a biological wilderness, not a recreational wilderness.

If it's like this for me, in my soft, privileged life—stressed between the two sides of a question and the two lives—what must it be like for the grizzlies and wolves?

A YOUNG WOMAN who had the great fortune to have been born here, and to grow up here, once asked me that question, the one about being quiet or speaking up. About being inactive or active. She was upset that I'd said the secret name of her home, my home, to the larger world—the name of this valley. She wanted to believe, I think, that things would stay the same and that voicelessness, not voice, was more honorable, as well as prudent.

She didn't agree with the abuses of the past, either, but wanted silence, just a little more silence, in the moment. I guess she assumed the future would take care of itself, or that the future turnings of the outside world would avoid

21

the valley or maybe even take care of things on the valley's behalf.

And maybe they will. But it has not been that way here in the past. My experience has been that the future devours. It does not protect.

This is not a place to come to. But it is a place to protect.

One year has turned into twenty-one, and counting. No one I respect could stand by and watch a landscape they love this much be damaged without raising a voice. My body and spirit are battered by twenty-plus years of the struggle, but my resolve is undiminished, firm and steady.

I would still like to know that these last roadless cores can be put out of harm's way, forever.

As soon as that's achieved, I'll get real quiet.

I'll walk into the dark woods and sit down.

I don't know what I'll feel. But I know that day will come. I just know it.

THE OLD MAN ON HIS BACK

Sharon Butala

SURELY THE YEARS FROM AGE SEVEN TO FIFTEEN or so, when my husband, Peter, rode his pony and then his horse, all by himself, in all kinds of weather, from his settler-family's tiny wooden house on the Old Man On His Back Plateau, five miles south and downhill across the rolling, grass-covered hills to the eight-grade, one-room schoolhouse at Divide (named after the continental divide that runs by there), and then back again at the end of the day, had a lot to do with his love for the prairie and its life and with his intimate knowledge of it.

It was a knowledge that only deepened as he grew to manhood and eventually to be sole owner of the ranch he'd been raised on. On his daylong rides patrolling fences and waterholes and caring for his cattle, he had gathered several bushels of the outer casings of the original buffalo horns scattered everywhere, all that was left of the original sixty million or so buffalo that once made the Great Plains of North America their home. Once, the bones of the buffalo, their skulls, and their horns had covered the prairie, but they had long ago been picked up by the homesteaders to sell as souvenirs and to buyers who crushed them to be used in the refining of sugar and for fertilizer—once a big, if short-lived, business.

But there was another reason that all those bones had disappeared: There is a famous picture at what, in 1882, would become the province of Saskatchewan's capital, Regina, but was then called Pile o' Bones, from the Cree *oskana kâ-asasteki,* of an enormous pile of buffalo bones, some of which had been gathered by the Indians, according to the *Encyclopedia of Saskatchewan,* "in the belief that the buffalo would not leave an area that contained the bones of their kind." This is why by the time Peter was born only the casings of their horns, dark brown, shaggy, and rough, were left scattered across the plains, hidden by the prairie grass and embedded in the thin, light soil, so that only the keen-eyed and knowledgeable could even find them.

Over time, Peter tells me, as he rode the prairie, he had come to dream of a return of the plains bison; he would probably say that he could not remember a time when he didn't imagine such a thing. In fact, I think that, at the very least, most born-and-bred Westerners dream of the time when the Great Plains and buffalo were virtually

synonymous. I mean "dream" in the sense of yearn to
have been there, to have seen the West when it was in a
pristine state and purely itself, before the arrival of Europeans. Even farmers and their families who, in their
government-sanctioned struggle to make a living, made
it impossible for the buffalo to return, must some morn-
ings rise and gaze, dreamy-eyed and half-asleep, across
their fields of wheat or canola or chick peas and summer
fallow, and imagine them to be, instead, all grass, dotted
with the hump-backed wild beasts. It isn't hard for some
Westerners to extend the dream of how the prairie once
was to imagining it that way once again—if only in a few
places—and available for all dreamers to visit to see that
astonishing past returned to life.

The Old Man On His Back Plateau, with an average altitude of about thirty-two hundred feet, is about
forty miles south of the famed Cypress Hills proper. It
is a small, grass-covered plateau, its western edge fewer
than thirty miles from the Alberta border and its eastern
edge about fifty miles from it. On the thirteen thousand
acres of mixed grass—all in one block—owned and managed by the Butalas, only twelve hundred acres had ever
been broken to the plow. All the rest was designated in a
Nature Conservancy of Canada report as being in "excellent condition," meaning that it was not overgrazed or
overrun by cactus, sage, or other "invaders," some of
which, such as crested wheatgrass, are not even native to
the Canadian prairie. It was as close to the grassland that

nineteenth-century explorers and fur traders would have seen (had they never crossed the plateau specifically, and there is no record that any did) as any grassland remaining in Canada.

As Peter aged and the physical toll of his way of life—broken bones from horse accidents, worn-out, arthritic joints from fifty or so years of forking hay or throwing eighty-pound square bales—made it impossible for him to continue ranching, his determination grew: He would find a way to retire without handing his much-loved grass over to men who would only plow it or who would break it into small acreages, each with a different owner, who, he was afraid, would then put too many cattle on it and destroy forever the beauty and purity it had cost him so much to preserve.

It took several years of searching, but, at last, together we found the Nature Conservancy of Canada, which, after a few more years, began negotiations with us and with the government of Saskatchewan to take over the ranch with the aim of preserving the grass. This was the first and most important goal, and although we barely whispered it to each other, all of us involved dreamt privately and together of maybe, just maybe, somehow, someday, putting the buffalo back on it, too. The land negotiation was a long, complicated process as nothing like this had ever been done in Saskatchewan before and the government, which held the deed to the large part of Butala land that was ours by lease, needed to be very careful in the way it went about establishing such a precedent. (Peter likes to say that the process took two years and five lawyers, but the negotiations were never unpleasant because, luckily for us, everybody involved wanted this to happen and worked in good faith toward it.) Finally, on July 18, 1996, the Old Man On His Back Prairie and Heritage Conservation Area was born.

Old Man On His Back is, of course, a translation of an aboriginal name. We knew this because that is the name on a Dominion of Canada map dated 1888, before there were settlers in this specific area. They didn't come here until about 1910, when all the best land opened for settlement elsewhere was gone and, especially, that most desirable land closest to the main railway line. It was a Cree elder who told us, when asked, that the place got its name because "long time ago we found an old man up there...in bad shape." Much later we found that the original story goes something like this: *Napi was in a battle and he was wounded so he lay down to rest. His blood flowed to the west and made the red sandstone cliffs of southeastern Alberta. His wounds were infected and the pus flowed to the east and made the white clay cliffs of southwestern Saskatchewan.* The "Old Man's" true name is Napi, and he is a cultural hero of the plains First Nations people that Euro-Canadians call the Blackfoot Nation. So, an archaeologist told us, explaining that when one people moved into another peoples' territory (as the Cree had done, moving west into Blackfoot territory as the buffalo began to disappear), they often adapted the first peoples' stories to their own lexicon, so that the Old Man of the Cree story was actually Napi. We Euro-Canadians have been ranching on, as local people refer to it casually in conversation, "the old man."

It is the sad fact that around 150 years ago, not only did Europeans claim Aboriginal land for themselves, for the most part with no or completely inadequate compensation, they introduced to the Great Plains an entirely new way of viewing land: as commodity, with the corollary of "useless" or else "useful." Surely the latter view bordered on blasphemy to the people native to the plains. Equally incomprehensibly to the First Nations, we also introduced the idea of land as private property, when for no one knows how many centuries it had been communal, regarded as a gift from the Creator. More, it was and is seen by the First Nations as not empty but fully inhabited, by Spirit: every rock, every tree, every blade of grass, every stream and pond and river. In addition, we soon co-opted some First Nations people into helping us depopulate it of birds and animals.

The awful result of our claiming the land for ourselves was that we not only took away the means of livelihood of an entire people, confining them to small and inadequate reserves and step by step taking away their rights as an independent people, but also took away, without even realizing we were doing it, something much more basic, much more profound. By taking away the land in which

28

the spiritual life of the people dwelt, and from which it emanated, we took away the entire basis of their culture. Or at least we tried our best to do so.

But the power of that original belief system is such that even under these onerous conditions "the people," as most Aboriginal peoples' name for themselves translates, retained that belief system, and today it is returning in its full force. Even more astonishing, some Euro-Canadians are, if not fully accepting these beliefs, at least intellectually are, with some chagrin, beginning to wonder if perhaps the First Nations' ideas about land were not always the right and best ones.

Probably, if there hadn't been this climate of reconsideration, we would have had a much harder time establishing our conserve. The dream had been to return the land to its "original" state—that is, its pre-settlement, postglacial state, the state that developed after the waters receded, the land dried, and the first great black spruce forest died away to leave behind grassland. After that was done, the dream was to bring back buffalo to live on it as they had before that vast, nearly total extinguishment in the late nineteenth century, so vast that historians wonder if there has ever been a comparable one anywhere on Earth.

29

That is why, that frigid December night when the twenty-five female and twenty-five male buffalo calves leaped cheerfully from the back of the stock trailers that had transported them from the Elk Island National Park, and their hooves touched the ground of the Old Man, something I can only characterize as euphoria—I write this without exaggeration, without posturing; it was indeed a euphoria—overcame every one of us there to see it. These were the descendants of the few of the original plains bison rescued by a handful of farseeing men around the turn of the century. They were DNA certified as having no cow genes, nor a single wood bison gene, but were *the real thing*. We all knew that although we shared a dream, and many people being paid salaries to bring this about had worked very hard to overcome the countless obstacles in the way, and many others had provided the large amount of money needed to make it all happen, we had been also dealing—unknown to us—with the revered Ancestors of the First Nations plains people who were there that night, too. As a Cree elder had said to me on the day we celebrated the establishment of the conservation area, "They—the Ancestors—are all around, and they are happy." How much happier they must have been the night the buffalo came back.

That night we did not merely say to the buffalo, "Welcome," but instead, "Welcome home." At the moment of their returning, awe was the only appropriate response— awe and overwhelming gratitude. But an Aboriginal man present, deeply moved, said to us of his people, "This gives them back their honor." Even though I think we mean something slightly different by our use of the word, I would say that perhaps, after nearly 150 years of shame, it also returns to us—we Euro-Canadians—some of ours.

WEB AROUND A TREE

Adrian Forsyth

NAKED EXCITEMENT SHONE ON JAVIER MENDOZA'S face. A hard-working, religious Costa Rican *campesino*, Javier is usually quite formal with me. He asks if we can fix a time to talk about how our tree-planting project on the Osa Peninsula is doing. Then he comes at the appointed time, sits, opens his notebook, and we talk. But on this day he impulsively ran up to me, eyes wide, and began talking excitedly about what he had found in the forest—some sort of very rare prized bird nest.

Javier has never been very excited by birds—fishing and keyboard music are his passions—so I found this behavior rather strange. We walked out into the forest to the base of a large *Carapa guianensis*, the tree popularly known as Royal Mahogany, or *Cedro bateo* to Javier. He gesticulated toward the upper trunk, twenty meters above our heads. It was hard for me to see what he was pointing out, but eventually I saw a strange and cryptic nest lying flat against the trunk like an inverted woven flask.

The nest was nearly identical in hue to the mottled gray lichen-covered *Carapa* bark. Its presence was betrayed only by a dark tubular opening just visible when viewed directly from below. Javier explained that any man who found such a nest could make himself irresistible to a woman by offering it to her. I subsequently learned that the nest was built from plant fibers by a lesser swallow-tailed swift, a tiny black-and-white bird of mercurial speed that zips about the forest feeding on flying ants and other insects. Swifts have weakly developed feet— they disdain to land on the ground or horizontal surfaces, preferring either the sky or a vertical surface. Their nests are among the most inaccessible in the world. Some species nest on cliff faces behind waterfalls; others nest deep in caves, where men routinely die or are injured while climbing to collect nests for the famed bird's nest soup concocted from these lumps of congealed swift spittle. In the case of the lesser swallow-tailed swift, it is romance that drives the men up tall trees.

Ornithologist Gary Stiles, author of the authoritative *Birds of Costa Rica,* records that "the nest, the bird, or any part of either are still regarded by some country folk as a powerful aphrodisiac (when appropriately prepared by the local witch, or brujo)." But who needs a witch? Possession of this nest would be credible evidence that a suitor

32

had keen powers of observation. Such a fellow would have to be a hell of a tree climber, and to be rather brave, for a *Carapa* tree does not offer easy access. As it climbs toward the sun, *Carapa* throws off its shaded lower limbs. Its trunk rises above its buttress as a straight column with no limbs to grasp. The climb would be risky. *Carapa* bark flakes off readily in circular plates, making the use of a fiber belt, the traditional tree-climber ascender, a dubious technology. The swift chooses its redoubt well—hence the power of the nest; the purveyor of this prize must pass muster as a determined suitor.

I wondered why this unusual expression of a country boy's ardor should be glued to this particular tree. *Carapa* was not the only choice the swallow had. Costa Rica's lush Osa Peninsula supports a bewildering richness of some seven hundred tree species. Right next to the *Carapa* were *Calophyllum* trees of equal stature, but their dark, deeply fissured bark supported yellow lichens offering lesser prospects for camouflage. Thinking of *Carapa*'s qualifications as a nesting site made me more attuned to this tree, and so for the past few years I have been observing *Carapa* trees whenever I am in their midst and making note of what happens on and around them. Any natural historian will attest that every forest is little explored and every tree is poorly understood. In that sense there is nothing, and everything, special about Carapa.

A falling *Carapa* fruit is a formidable object. The size of a grapefruit, it is firmly solid, and the heavy clay roof tile on my house is sometimes shattered when a gust of wind carries one laterally and down. I rate these fruits up there with coconuts as hazards to mental health. But these characteristics enable *Carapa* to produce a highly successful seed crop. A crashing Carapa fruit pod breaks open in quarters, throwing seeds willy-nilly about the forest floor. Normally one finds eight large, distinctively shaped seeds per pod. Imagine slicing a sphere vertically with two cuts—one east-west, the other north-south—and then bisecting the sphere with a horizontal cut through the equatorial plane. A seed shape with a round outer section and three flat right-angled planes is the result. The seeds are larger than chestnuts or Ping-Pong balls and can weigh as much as sixty grams.

A mature *Carapa* tree can throw down two hundred kilos of seeds in a good year, providing a huge food resource for seed-eating rodents such as agoutis, which gather and hoard the seeds. Buried seeds are more likely to escape the attention of competitors, including the peccary pigs that root through the leaf litter. Buried seeds are also protected from attack by pyralid moths, which lay their eggs in *Carapa* seeds. A *Carapa* seed left exposed normally becomes a miniature ecosystem of caterpillars, assorted fly larvae, and beetles, which all reduce the seed to frass, and no tree will result. *Carapa* thus depends on the forgetfulness of agoutis and the reasonable chance that after an agouti buries a store of *Carapa* seeds they will be eaten by an ocelot or other cat and new trees will grow.

The *Carapa* are thickest always at the escarpment above the sea at the bottom of a series of ridges that drain from the central elevated spine of the Osa land mass. I always thought this concentration occurred because *Carapa* likes its feet damp but not sodden; it is never common on drier ridges. But there may be more than this preference affecting its concentration along the coast. Land crabs such as *Geocarcinus* dominate the vegetation for hundreds of meters in from the sea. *Geocarcinus* is a handsome stout crab. Its forelimbs are a bright reddish purple, and the rest of the legs are a yellow-orange, in stark contrast to its heavy purple-black carapace. *Geocarcinus* will eat meat, but the mainstay of its diet is plant material, fallen leaves, and tender long seedlings. When a tree seed sprouts, there is a good chance a crab will eat it. But buried *Carapa* seeds have huge food reserves. In a couple of days, a germinating seed can send up a strong stalk carrying its first leaves and growing shoots above the reach of the crabs, giving it a considerable advantage over trees with lesser resources. Crabs may promote the dominance of *Carapa* along the coast.

There are many more strands in this web of interactions around *Carapa* seeds. For example, the crabs are held in check somewhat by coatimundis. Coatis, relatives of raccoons with a stretched-out nose and black-and-white candy-cane tail, prefer turtle eggs above all else. But in the dry season, when the turtles are not nesting, the coatis pound the *Geocarcinus* crab population. Cats such as puma, jaguar, and ocelots eat coatis and agoutis. How does the cats' presence affect this tree? Eating an agouti increases the number of seeding sprouts, but eating a coati increases the number of crabs. It is hard to imagine how questions about the interdependence of these animals with the trees could be reasonably answered except to say that crabs, *Carapa*, coatis, and cats have all coexisted for hundreds of thousands of years and their lives are intertwined.

Humans affect *Carapa* in two obvious ways. The first is to usurp the consumers of the seeds. *Carapa* seeds are harvested for their oil. The seed kernel contains 56 percent liquid oil, of a transparent yellow color, that solidifies to a consistency of vaseline at temperatures below 25°C. You don't eat it or cook with it, because like all parts of the plant, it's incredibly bitter. This bitterness is attributed to a group of terpene chemicals called meliacins, which are very similar in structure and effectiveness to other antimalarial chemicals found in other tropical plants, such as quinine.

Andiroba oil, as *Carapa* seed oil is called in the Amazon, is widely used. Indigenous peoples in the Amazon mix andiroba with the red pigment extracted from annatto seeds and rub the oily paste all over their bodies and even into their hair to protect themselves from biting flies. This oil was used as a lamp fuel in the early 1800s, even in large cities such as Belem. It burns with little smoke, but it also repels pests. Today Brazilian city dwellers use andiroba oil to treat arthritis and to cure infections and fungal skin diseases and also as a massage oil. Chemical analysis of andiroba oil, bark, and leaves reveals the presence of another group of chemicals called limonoids, which contribute anti-inflammatory and insect repellent properties to andiroba oil. The oil is also used in Brazil as a furniture polish that is thought to protect wooden furniture from termites and other wood-chewing insects. On the Osa, people give little thought to the oil, but they do use the timber.

Carapa wood has natural resistance to decay and wood-boring insects. It is reasonably popular for making items such as doors, but calling this wood Royal Mahogany is more of a marketing ploy than a reflection of any resemblance to the big-leafed mahogany prized by furniture makers. They are both members of the same plant family. But unlike mahogany, which carves and saws butter smooth, *Carapa* saws wooly, and it lacks the rich brown color of true mahogany. Perhaps that is why mahogany is virtually extinct in the wild but *Carapa* soldiers on.

I watched some woodworking with a *Carapa* recently. Parrots, not people, did the carving. During my last visit to the Osa, I watched a pair of scarlet macaws prospecting a *Carapa* limb scar. Macaws are renowned for their huge shearing recurved bills. After pulling off the bark, they began excavating a nest cavity. *Carapa* wood is about as dense as oak. Seeing it shredded and pulled away in chunks and strips with apparent ease gave me respect for the bite of these birds. Whenever another pair of macaws flew by, the pair working on my *Carapa* called loudly and raucously in seeming discouragement of potential interlopers. Some biologists think that the very strong pairing of macaws and their gaudy plumage may be the result of strong selection for male-female pairs to jointly defend a nest and to advertise their competence and willingness to do battle. This pair certainly did not seem about to cede their *Carapa* tree without a fight.

They took their time making up their minds about which tree to occupy. They flew from one *Carapa* tree to another, considering three *Carapa* above all the other trees in the area. They excavated cavities in all three and spent a lot of time going in and out of them. Perhaps they hedge their bets but always have several sites to use. It was then, watching the macaws, that I began to imagine another possible connection woven round *Carapa*. The trade in macaw chicks is ancient. People have been robbing macaw nests for millennia. Indigenous people first, then pirates, and now modern-day wildlife poachers and their urban clients have all prized these gaudy birds. It seems highly likely that a parrot poacher climbing preferred nesting trees such as *Carapa* would have encountered the curious woven nest of the lesser swallow-tailed swift and carried it back as a *memento macho* from his daring excursion to the heights of the forest. Perhaps then a custom was born, a tendril of a connection extended from tree to bird to human to another bird.

Not that we will soon know the truth of such specu-
lations. Few of the ecological connections that do exist
have been documented, much less verified by experimental hypothesis testing. These poorly studied forests
and the thousands of little known trees species that they
harbor are daily diminished by logging and land clear-
ing. So too in a rapidly urbanizing world the knowledge
of these trees and forest that resides with people such as
Javier grows smaller. The privilege and challenge of our
ecological awakening to realize we still scarcely comprehend the basic natural history of most species. If we are
ever to know what is true ecological sustainability, we
must gather that knowledge as fast as we are able.

THE REAL STUFF

—— *Richard Mabey* ——

I'M INCREASINGLY TROUBLED BY HOW, AT THE BEGIN-
ning of the twenty-first century, the science of life is once
again having to defend itself against religion. You'd have
thought that, 150 years on from the first agonizings over
Darwinism, we would all have accepted that evolution
was a more intricate and beautiful process than anything
that could be dreamed of by a mystic, that life was wonderful, exciting, fulfilling in itself. Complete. But once
again we're told there must be "more to life." Some reason
for it all, some purpose. And it is not just the orthodoxly
religious who seem needy for metaphysical explanations.
As someone who writes about nature in ways that I hope
are lyrical and metaphorical as well as descriptive, I often
find that my readers—inquisitive and scientifically liter-
ate folk for the most part—assume that I must have some
"spiritual" interest in nature. I'm not sure I know what they

mean by this term, but I think it has to do with believing in something "behind" or "beyond" the physical surface of things. Some truth that is greater or more significant than can be extracted by the mechanical investigations of science. I'm sorry to disappoint them and feel that I must sound like an agent of the enemy when I confess to being an intense and passionate materialist.

But I do understand the experiences of nature that can generate awe and even incredulity and perhaps stir those wonderings about something "beyond" nature, some greater order. Recently, via television in England, we've had the opportunity to witness what is perhaps the most extraordinary wildlife spectacle on the planet. Every winter dusk, out in the emptiness of the marshlands of southwest England, more than a million starlings home in on a patch of reeds in Somerset for their nightly roost. They stream in from the countryside beyond, an endless flow of quivering black scribbles, joining, breaking ranks, floating free. Suddenly, they become plasmic, one immense organism, pulsating like a single cell. They have the look of a dark, swirling Aurora. They swing up to the sky and then skim the reeds in folds and falls of black. They fill out great parabolas and helixes, with a symmetry you do not expect from living things. Then, birds again, they fall into the reeds. It is mysterious and transfixing and still beyond understanding. It may result from minute, reciprocal movements by each single bird to preserve its flight space, which makes the flock behave something like a gas or a fluid. But no cloud formation or rushing river

41

ever revealed such exquisite mutable geometry, and we are left asking those scientifically unanswerable questions: "What it is it for? What does it mean?"

EXPERIENCES LIKE THIS are supposed to fill even the godless among us with intimations of the spiritual. To give us a glimpse of the universal geometry that lies behind the chaos of life, of the workings of a group consciousness outside anything we can imagine. The trouble for me is that I know these birds away from their dusk rites. They're some way from being aerial ectoplasm. They're urchins, opportunists, prodigious mimics. Mozart had a pet starling, which famously learned a theme from his G Major piano concerto but jumped it forward a couple of centuries by changing the G-natural to a G-sharp. And, like all living creatures, the birds are victims, too. I once saw, too close for comfort, a starling being dismembered by a sparrowhawk. The starling's beak was wide open, not to utter a G-sharp or even a scream, but because it was being slowly squeezed to death. No moral context for these birds, no more blame on the hawk for being what it is than on the starling for being weaker and slower and so very edible. No sacrifice of the self for some higher significance—unless joining the great chain of dependence is itself a kind of sacrament.

It's always been like this for me with spirituality. I catch a whiff of the numinous, and it turns visceral in a moment, part of the digestive process. The first time was when I was a teenager. I fell into a state of thraldom to

42

the hill above our house. It wasn't a particularly special hill, just a chalk swell that looked out over a wooded valley and a thin winterbourne that, according to local legend, was a woe-water, which flowed only in time of trouble. But I thought it was the most achingly beautiful prospect I had ever seen. It haunted me with some not quite graspable meaning, like the image of the mountain in *Close Encounters of the Third Kind*. It was an unsettling feeling, edgy, indefinable, a mixture of exquisite pleasure and butterfly discomfort. At times it turned into an actual physical sensation that made the back of my legs clench, as if I were peering down from a great height. I experienced the same ethereal feelings singing medieval carols with the school choir in the lamplit porches of the big houses at the edge of our town, and then at the ritual reading of Chapter 13 of St. Paul's Epistle to the Corinthians at the end of term: "When I was a child I spake as a child ... but when I became a man I put away childish things." I hadn't the slightest interest in the religious content of these ancient texts, but they seemed like a bridge across time, a fleeting glimpse of something inexpressibly bigger than the shackling routines of school, perhaps a first intimation of the continuity of life. If any of these blurrily romantic feelings had depths beyond that, I guess they were in Deep England, which was beginning to cast its dubious aura over me.

43

Then, about ten years later, something different. I was trying to navigate my way through the last stages of a long anxiety attack, to get through the "glass wall" such states erect between you and reality. I was suddenly struck by a piercing moment of heightened perception, as if a lens had been clamped over my eye. I was convinced I could pick out the minute physical details of the world nearly a quarter of a mile away: individual bricks, a man's ears, the discrete eddies in a plume of smoke. Of course, I'd simply become aware of part of the sensory processing that I performed unselfconsciously every second of my life. But it seemed, in that moment of hypersensitivity, to be some inexplicable, supernatural gift. It looked as if "the beyond," for me, was always going to be just a few hundred yards away.

But the eye—that ought to have made me pause. For the religiously inclined, it's not only the mirror of the soul but a kind of portal to the mysteries beyond evolution. For decades it was thought to be the blind spot in Darwin's theory. How, even over thousands of millions of years, could any living structure of such extraordinary complexity have been developed by chance mutations? How could it all—the light-sensitive iris, the nerve transmitters in the retina, the lens, the lids, the tears—how could it all be *coordinated* as well?

Anne Stevenson's poem about a new baby ponders the origins of the eyelashes and their connected capillaries and nerves. She calls the poem "The Spirit is too Blunt an Instrument." And God perhaps too exact a watchmaker. What is clear from the increasingly extraordinary revelations about the intricacy of the living world is that

44

Intelligent Design is a logical impossibility. It's not that God isn't clever enough but that life isn't that kind of process. The Reverend Paley's vision of the living world as an exquisitely engineered watch is as inappropriate as seeing Creation as a symphony unfolding from a written score. What it *is* like is a vast piece of musical improvisation, unpredictable, free-form, exuberant, brilliantly inventive, yet melding exquisitely with what already exists (anything that doesn't fit rapidly disappears). And, like all such music, quite without meaning, just gloriously itself.

ISN'T THIS SOMETHING to have faith in? The *stuff* of life, the astonishing, resilient, surreal inventiveness of it all? The extravagant iridescence in the wings of butterflies? The minute convolutions of Henle's loops in the human kidneys, "like the meanders in a creek"? The song of the Albert's lyrebird, which takes it six years to learn and includes the phrasing of every other bird in the Queensland bush? The *blood* of the bar-headed goose, which enables it to fly over the Himalayas? At times the gratuitousness of creation, its sheer wild playfulness, can only be understood as a kind of unscripted comedy.

Long before I knew much about the fantastic domestic arrangements that are the norm for life in the tropics, I learned about the transactions of Britain's rarest butterfly, the large blue. Its larvae feed for a while on wild thyme and start producing honey on their abdomens. They also produce a pheromone that mimics the scent of ant grubs.

45

The adult ants gather up the butterfly larvae, take them off to their nests, and look after them as if they were their own offspring—drinking their honey in return. All the while the larvae sing to the ants, echoing the rhythmic noises of the grubs. Wouldn't it have been simpler, Annie Dillard inquires in her rodeo ride of God in *Pilgrim at Tinker Creek,* "just to rough in a slab of chemicals, a green acre of goo? . . . The lone ping into being of the first hydrogen atom *ex nihilo* was so unthinkable, violently radical, that surely it ought to have been enough. But look what happens. You open the door and all heaven and hell break loose." Wouldn't it have been easier, for that matter, to have nothing at all, no lone hydrogen atom, no first cause? The fact that there is *anything* is the one impenetrable mystery. Once there was, the eventual emergence of the planet's grand comedy of manners was pretty well inevitable.

Once in an interview, trying again to sidestep those inevitable queries about spirituality, I suggested that I could be described as a "*transcendental* materialist." I was posing a bit and should have had the guts to call myself a straightforward materialist. But what I was trying to say was that, for me, the physicality of the living world— its truthfulness, its anciently involved intelligence, its wit, its refusal to be pinned down—transcends itself into the realm not of the supernatural but of the hyperreal. The true Transcendentalists in nineteenth-century America believed almost the exact opposite, arguing, anthropocentrically, that the material world was a product of some mystical, ideal force. "Nature is the incarnation of thought," wrote Ralph Waldo Emerson, their guru, in *Nature*. "The world is mind precipitated." Emerson's friend Thoreau called himself a transcendentalist but was altogether more grounded. His epic climb up into the desolate wilderness of Mount Katahdin is the seminal statement about the absolute authority of the physical: "Talk of mysteries! Think of our life in nature,—daily to be shown matter, to come into contact with it,—rocks, trees, wind on our cheeks! The *solid* earth! The *actual* world! The *common sense! Contact! Contact!*" In *Walden*, less frenziedly, Thoreau writes about measuring the depth of his pond. It's a passage that is both literal and metaphorical, about reality and responsibility: "The greatest depth was exactly one hundred and two feet; to which may be added the five feet I had risen since, making one hundred and seven. This is a remarkable depth for so small an area; yet not one inch of it can he spared by the imagination . . . While some men believe in the infinite some ponds will be thought to be bottomless." The imagination, he is suggesting, needs detail and finitude, not abstraction, for its full flowering.

My own bottomless pond is the mystery of self-consciousness, a phenomenon that I suspect is no more open to "explanation" than the fact that something came to exist. Pondering it when I was young was another vertiginous experience. If the sense of self was a product of

47

the processes of the brain, could there be another "me" somewhere else, where the immense possibilities of the universe had thrown up an identical physical being? And if I couldn't be a self in two places at once, could I be so in two different times? Might brain chemistry be the answer to reincarnation?

Thankfully I grew out of tormenting myself with unanswerable questions, but the self remains the chink in the materialist's armour. And on a very few occasions, I've had the feeling that I suppose is the one thing common to all so-called spiritual experiences, that its boundaries are relaxing a little. One May night especially, listening to nightingales in Suffolk, was something close to a moment of communion. The setting was narcotic. A full moon, mounds of cow parsley glowing like suspended balls of mist, the fen arching like a lustrous whaleback across the whole span of the southern horizon. The nightingale was a shaman, experienced, rhetorical, insistent. I sank into its charms, a willing initiate. A shooting star arced over the bush in which it was singing. As I edged closer, its song seemed to become solid, to be doing odd things to the light. I was aware that my peripheral vision was closing down, and that I had no sense of where I was in space. And then, for just a few seconds, the bird was in my head, and it was I who was singing.

Conventionally, one is supposed to feel awe and humility at moments like this. Not a bit of it. Awe seems to me an appropriate emotion for God, viewing the exuberance of the living world from a distance. But not for a creature caught up in it. I was part of the home team, on the winning side, fist in the air, cheering in solidarity. Nor did I feel that my self had shrunk, or grown insignificant, but rather that the bird and I and landscape were at that moment part of a larger being.

It's telling how often music is the agency for such experiences and a metaphor for what they mean. The great American biologist Lewis Thomas has written often of the sensory communications that keep the planet working harmoniously, of signals "informing tissues in the vegetation of the Alps about the state of eels in the Sargasso Sea." He once imagined what it might be like if we could hear the planet's "grand canonical ensemble," if we could make out vibrations of a million locusts in migration, the descants of whales, the timpani of gorilla breasts, termite heads, drumfish bladders. The combined sound might be a sacred oratorio that would lift us off our feet.

RISE UP

and RECLAIM

Environmentalists are not against

everything; they are for the most important

things on this planet, things that keep

us alive and wealthy. They are for clear air,

clean water, clean soil, and a diversity of creatures

all over the world. Environmentalists work

for local communities that are sustainable,

for economics in which full employment, security,

and spiritual needs are paramount.

And as they work to protect wilderness areas,

they celebrate the wondrous variety of life-forms

that share the planet with us.

{ DAVID SUZUKI }

MY CREDO

Helen Caldicott

I BELIEVE THAT WOMEN HOLD THE FATE OF THE Earth in the palm of their hands. Some 53 percent of us are women, and we are pretty wimpish. The majority of people who run politics, corporations, religions, and all other worldly affairs are men. Those women who do work are still not paid salaries equal to those of men. We don't step up to the plate—it's time we asserted our rights and took over. Men have had their turn, and we're in a profound mess. France has a new law decreeing that 50 percent of people running for politics must be women. This policy needs to be emulated by all countries in the world.

I believe that money is the root of all evil. When people start believing that materialism will produce ultimate, lasting happiness, it is a sure sign that they will be intensely unhappy. Many Americans are on antidepressants because they worship at the altar of materialism.

They should be lifting their souls, not their faces. True and lasting happiness lies in serving, not taking.

I believe the truth of the Einstein quote—"the splitting of the atom changed everything save man's mode of thinking, thus we drift towards unparalleled catastrophe." I believe that nuclear weapons still pose the greatest threat to life on Earth—Russia and the United States own 97 percent of the thirty-thousand H-bombs in the global arsenal, and they still target each other. I believe that nuclear power poses a threat to all future generations. Nuclear waste will enter food chains and over time induce epidemics of malignancy and genetic disease for all future generations of humans, animals, and plants. I believe that if we do not eliminate nuclear weapons and nuclear power, life on Earth will end with either a bang or a whimper.

I believe in the sanctity of nature. I believe we can save the planet. We are smart enough to do that, but we must act with a sense of dire emergency. The Earth is in the intensive care unit, we have an acute clinical emergency, and we are all now physicians to this dying planet. It can be saved, but only with the dedication and passion exemplified by passionate and dedicated physicians.

54

I believe that the media are controlling and determining the face of the Earth. As Thomas Jefferson said, an informed democracy will behave in a responsible fashion. We need to rise up and reclaim the airwaves, which have been hijacked by avaricious corporations to advance their profit margins. The airwaves are public property.

I believe in the beauty of classical music. I must have it; it feeds my soul. Beautiful music could unite all peoples on Earth and inspire them to commit their lives to saving the Earth for their children, their grandchildren, and all their descendents.

I believe in the goodness in every person's soul, even though it's sometimes hard to see. I treat a lot of patients when either their children are dying or they are dying. Even though sometimes it's heavily obscured, in extremes this goodness will emerge like a slowly opening rosebud.

I don't believe in a god. I have helped many people to die and believe that it's ashes to ashes and dust to dust. Who and where were we before conception? It will be the same when we die. It takes much more strength and courage to face the finality of the death of the ego than it does to believe in everlasting life.

I believe that heaven and hell are present every day. Life is what we make it. We are born alone and we die alone. Once this truth is accepted, one finds the strength to face and to overcome any adversity that life presents.

I believe that life is an absolute gift to be treasured accordingly. We are very privileged to even have been conceived. Of all the millions of genetically different sperm that my beloved father produced on the night of my conception, only my sperm reached my egg. What luck! What a miracle to be forever savored.

I believe that we are here to serve. We are not here to make ourselves happy, to be self-indulgent, or to be hedonistic. The happiest state that I achieve is when I work in my clinic helping my children with cystic fibrosis to face death, helping to treat them and to look after their siblings. I'm utterly exhausted at the end of the day but deeply, deeply fulfilled. I feel the same way when I give an inspirational lecture and change hundreds of lives, perhaps forever.

I believe in the beauty of my garden. I've got 2½ acres, and I'm never more in touch with the power of the universe than when I'm in my garden on a warm, sunny day tending to my flowers and my trees, with the pelicans circling overhead, the perfumes of jasmine and roses mingling with the smell of eucalypts. That for me is heaven.

I believe that there are far too many people on the planet. In 1900 there were one billion of us in the world. Now there are 6.5 billion, and the prediction is that within a few decades there will be 14 billion. We have to stop breeding like flies. We are not the most important species on Earth. Rather, I would say that we are ardently anthropocentric and are the most destructive species ever to grace the surface of planet Earth. If women are educated, if they are supplied with contraceptives and their standard of living is elevated, they stop reproducing. This is the secret that needs to be implemented to curb uncontrolled human fecundity.

56

I believe that the greatest terror in the world is not a few terrorists destroying the World Trade Center. It's the fact that half the world's people still live in dire poverty and thirty thousand to forty thousand children die every day from malnutrition and starvation, while the rich nations continue to get richer and richer. Two percent of the Earth's people own more than 50 percent of the wealth. This is obscene. How many chandeliers, cars, or houses can one person own? Many of these people claim to be Christians, yet it was Jesus who said that it is more difficult for a rich man to enter the kingdom of heaven than to pass through the eye of a needle.

I believe that the most important job in the world is mothering. Women need to be financially supported for it. Their job is far more important than that of chief executive officers at the head of huge corporations. Once again, if women do not assert themselves, they and their work will always be taken for granted. The magic number is 30 percent. Below this representation in government, women tend to vote to please the men. Above 30 percent representation, there is such mutual reinforcement that women say, "We're not voting for missiles today, we're voting for milk for children." And this change of tune bears no relationship to political leanings. It comes straight from the nurturing instincts triggered by the physiological dynamics of the estrogen and oxytocin receptors in the central nervous system.

I believe that the secret of happiness comes from (a) serving our fellow human beings and loving and caring for everyone (I don't mean crappy Californian love but really deep caring for each other, (b) understanding our own psychology in a profound way so that each of us can be a more constructive human being, and (c) caring for this incredible planet of ours.

THE ECOLOGIST

Paul Hawken

OVER THE PAST FIFTEEN YEARS, I HAVE GIVEN nearly a thousand talks about the environment, and every time I have felt like a tightrope performer struggling to maintain perfect balance. To be sure, people are interested to know what is happening to their world, but no speaker wants to leave an audience depressed, no matter how frightening the future may seem according to studies that predict the rate of environmental loss. To be sanguine about the future, however, requires a plausible basis for constructive action: you cannot describe possibilities for that future unless the present problem is accurately defined. Bridging the chasm between hope and depression was always a challenge, but audiences kindly ignored my intellectual vertigo and over time provided me with ways to overcome this challenge. After every speech a smaller crowd would gather to talk, ask questions, and exchange business cards. These people were typically working on the most salient issues of our day: climate change, poverty, deforestation, peace, water, hunger, conservation, human rights. They were students, grandmothers, teenagers, tribal members, businesspeople, architects, teachers, retired professors, and worried mothers and fathers.

I would get from five to thirty such cards per speech and, after being on the road for a week or two, would return home with a few hundred of them stuffed into various pockets. Over the years the number of cards mounted into the thousands, and whenever I glanced at them, I came back to one question: did anyone truly appreciate how many groups and organizations were engaged in progressive causes? At first this was a matter of curiosity, but it slowly grew into a hunch that something larger was afoot, a significant social movement that was eluding the radar of mainstream culture.

Intrigued, I began to count. I looked at government records for different countries, and, using various methods to approximate the number of environmental and social justice groups from tax census data, I initially estimated a total of 30,000 environmental organizations around the globe. When I added social justice and indigenous peoples' rights organizations, the number exceeded 100,000. I then researched to see if there had ever been any equal to this movement in scale or scope, but I couldn't find anything, past or present. The more I probed, the more organizations I unearthed, and the numbers continued to climb as I discovered lists, indexes, and small databases specific to certain sectors or geographic areas. In trying to pick up a stone, I found the exposed tip of a much larger geological formation. I soon realized that my initial estimate of 100,000 organizations was off by at least a factor of ten, and I now believe there are over one—and maybe even two—million organizations around the world working toward ecological sustainability and social justice.

By any conventional definition, this vast collection of committed individuals does not constitute a movement. Movements have leaders and ideologies. People *join* movements, study their tracts, and identify themselves with a group. They read the biography of the founder(s) or listen to them perorate on tape or in person. Movements, in short, have followers. This movement, however, doesn't fit the standard model. It is dispersed, inchoate, and fiercely independent. It has no manifesto or doctrine, no overriding authority to check with. It is taking shape in schoolrooms, farms, fields, jungles, villages, companies, deserts, fisheries, slums—and yes, even fancy hotel conference centers. One of the distinctive features is that it is tentatively emerging as a global humanitarian movement arising from the bottom up.

Historically, social movements have arisen primarily in response to injustice, inequities, and corruption.

Those woes still remain, joined by a new condition that has no precedent: the planet has a life-threatening disease, marked by massive ecological degradation and rapid climate change. As I counted these vast numbers of organizations, it crossed my mind that perhaps I was witnessing the growth of something organic, if not biologic. Rather than a movement in the conventional sense, could it be an instinctive, collective response to threat? Is it atomized for reasons that are innate to its purpose? How does it function? How fast is it growing? How is it connected? Why is it largely ignored? Does it have a history? Can it successfully address the issues that governments are failing to do: energy, jobs, conservation, poverty, and global warming?

I sought a name for the movement, but none exists. I met people who wanted to structure or organize it—a difficult task, since it would easily be the most complex association of human beings ever assembled. Many outside the movement criticize it as powerless, but that assessment does not stop its growth. When describing it to politicians, academics, and businesspeople, I found that many believe they are already familiar with this movement, how it works, what it consists of, and approximately how big it is. They base their conclusion on media reports about Amnesty International, the Sierra Club, Oxfam, or other venerable institutions. They may be directly acquainted with a few smaller organizations and may even sit on the board of a local group. For them and others, the movement is small and circumscribed, a new type of charity, with a sprinkling of ragtag activists who occasionally give it a bad name. People inside the movement can also underestimate it, basing their judgment on just the organizations they are linked to, even though their networks can only encompass a fraction of the whole. But after spending years researching this phenomenon, including creating with my colleagues a global database of its constituent organizations, I have come to this conclusion: this is the largest social movement in all of history. No one knows its scope, and how it functions is more mysterious than what meets the eye.

When I discuss the movement with academics or friends in the media, the first question they pose is usually the same: if it is so large, why isn't this movement more visible? By that they mean, why isn't it more visible to news media, especially TV? Although global in its scope, the movement generally remains unseen until it gathers to take part in demonstrations, whether in London, Prague, or New York, or at annual meetings of the World Social Forum, after which it seems to disappear again, reinforcing the perception that it is a will-o'-the-wisp. The movement doesn't fit neatly into any category in modern society, and what can't be visualized can't be named. In business, what isn't measured isn't managed; in the media, what isn't visible isn't reported. Media coverage of the death of Pope John Paul and the election of Pope Benedict easily surpassed all coverage devoted to this movement over the past ten years, yet the number of people directly working and indirectly involved with the movement is greater than the number of people active in the Catholic Church. The papacy has history and specificity; the movement is about the future.

Picture the collective presence of all human beings as an organism. Pervading that organism are intelligent activities, humanity's immune response to resist and heal the effects of political corruption, economic disease, and ecological degradation. In a world grown too complex for constrictive ideologies, even the very word *movement* to describe such a process may be limiting. Writer and activist Naomi Klein calls it "the movement of movements," but for lack of a better term I will stick with *movement* here because I believe all its components are beginning to converge.

The movement has three basic roots: environmental activism, social justice initiatives, and indigenous cultures' resistance to globalization, all of which have become intertwined. Collectively, it expresses the needs of the majority of people on Earth to sustain the environment, wage peace, democratize decision making and policy, reinvent public governance piece by piece from the bottom up, and improve their lives—women, children, and the poor.

This movement is not bound together by an "-ism." What unifies it is ideas, not ideologies. There is a vast difference between the two; ideas question and liberate, whereas ideologies justify and dictate. One of the differences between the bottom-up movement now erupting around the world and established ideologies is that the movement develops its ideas based on observation, whereas ideologies act on the basis of belief or theory. Are there ideologues in the movement? To be sure, but fundamentally the movement is that part of humanity that has assumed the task of protecting and saving itself. If we accept that the metaphor of an organism can be applied to humankind, we can imagine a collective movement that would protect, repair, and restore that organism's capacity to endure when threatened. If so, that capacity to respond would function like an immune system, which operates independently of an individual person's intent.

Just as the immune system is the line of internal defense that allows an organism to persist over time, sustainability is a strategy for humanity to continue to exist over time. The word *immunity* comes from the Latin *im munis*, meaning "ready to serve." The immune system is usually portrayed in militaristic terms: a biological defense department armed to fight off invading organisms. In the textbook case, antibodies attach themselves to molecular invaders, which are then neutralized and destroyed by white blood cells. Simple and elegant, but the process of fending off invaders and disease is more complex and interesting.

The immune system is the most diverse system in the body, consisting of an array of proteins, immunoglobulins,

64

monocytes, macrophages, and more, a microbestiary of cells working in sync with one another, without which we would perish in a matter of days, like a rotten piece of fruit, devoured by billions of viruses, bacilli, fungi, and parasites, to whom we are a juicy lunch wrapped in jeans and T-shirt. The immune system is everywhere, dispersed in lymphatic fluid, which courses through the thymus, the spleen, and the thousands of lymph nodes scattered like little peanuts throughout the body.

At the core of immunity is a miracle of recovery and restoration, for there are times when our immune system is weakened. Stress, chemicals, infections, lack of sleep, and poor diets can overwhelm the immune system and send it into a tailspin. When that happens, old diseases can resurface while protection from new ones breaks down. Pathogens burgeon and seem to hold sway, and a moment comes when death lurks at the threshold. At that point, given the odds and circumstances, something extraordinary can happen that really shouldn't: the immunological descent slows and halts, our life hangs in the balance, and we begin to heal, a comeback that rivals the climax of a Hollywood plot. How the disoriented and muddled immune system reverses course and recovers is not well understood; some would say it is a mystery.

The workings of this immune system sound orderly and precise, but they are not. Antibodies bind not just to pathogens but to many types of cells, even themselves, as if the lymphatic system were a chamber-of-commerce mixer of local business owners feverishly exchanging business cards. In *The Web of Life,* Fritjof Capra writes, "The entire system looks much more like a network, more like the Internet than soldiers looking out for an enemy. Gradually, immunologists have been forced to shift their perception from an immune system to an immune network." Francesco Varela and Antonio Coutinho describe an immune system that can best be understood as intelligence, a living, learning, self-regulating system—almost another mind. Its function does not depend on its firepower but on the quality of its connectedness. Rather than "inside cells" automatically destroying "outside cells," there is a mediatory response to pathogens, as if the immune system learned millions of years ago that détente and getting to know potential adversaries was wiser than first-strike responses, that achieving balance was more appropriate than eradication. The immune system depends on its diversity to maintain resiliency, with which it can maintain homeostasis, respond to surprises, learn from pathogens, and adapt to sudden changes. The implication for medicine is clear: to fend off cancer and infection, we may need to understand how to increase the immune network's connectivity rather than the intensity of its response.

Similarly, the widely diverse network of organizations proliferating in the world today may be a better defense against injustice than F-16 fighter jets. Connectivity allows these organizations to be task-specific and focus their resources precisely and frugally. Incremental success is achieved by consensus operating within informal structures, where no one person has all or much power. The force that such groups exert is in the form of dialogue and truthfulness. Computers, cell phones, broadband, and the Internet have created perfect conditions for the network to unify.

According to Kevin Kelly, author of *Out of Control*, the Internet already consists of a quintillion transistors, a trillion links, and a million e-mails per second. Moore's Law, which predicts that processing power will double in power and halve in price every eighteen months, is meeting Metcalfe's Law, which states that the usefulness of a network grows exponentially with arithmetic increases in numbers of users. These laws enable big corporations as much as they do small NGOs, but the latter gain greater advantage because these new technologies amplify smallness more effectively than largeness. Large organizations don't need networks; small ones thrive on them. Webs are complex systems of interconnected elements that link individual actions to larger grids of knowledge and movement. Web sites link to other sites with more links to other sites ad infinitum, creating a critical, fluid mass of information that evolves and grows as needed—very much like the response of our immune systems. At the heart of all of this is not technology but relationships, tens of millions of people working toward restoration and social justice.

67

THE STATE OF the world today suggests that given the number of organizations and people dedicated to fighting injustice, the movement has not been particularly effective. The counterargument to this claim is that globalization's depredations have had a nearly five-hundred-year head start on humanity's immune system. The exponential assault on resources and the production of waste, coupled with the extirpation of cultures and the exploitation of workers, is a disease as surely as hepatitis or cancer is. It is caused by a political-economic system of which we are all a part, and any finger-pointing is inevitably directed back to ourselves. There may be no particular *they* there, but the system is still a disease, even if we created and contracted it. Because a lot of people know we are sick and want to treat the cause, not just the symptoms, the environmental movement is humanity's response to contagious policies that are killing the Earth, while the social justice movement addresses economic and political pathogens that destroy families, bodies, cultures, and communities. They are two sides of the same coin, because when you harm one you harm the other. They address what Dr. Paul Farmer calls the "pathologies of power," the "rising tide of inequalities" that breed violence, whether it be to people, ecosystems, or other forms of life. No government can say it cares for its citizens while allowing the environment to be trashed.

The ultimate purpose of a global immune system is to identify what is not life affirming and to contain, neutralize, or eliminate it. Where communities, cultures, and ecosystems have been damaged, it seeks to prevent additional harm and then heal and restore the damage. Most social-change organizations are understaffed and underfunded, and nearly all are negotiating steep learning curves. It is not easy to create a system that has no antecedent, and if you study the taxonomy of the movement, you will see a new curriculum for humankind emerging, some of it corrective, some of it restorative, and some of it highly imaginative.

In many countries participation in the movement can be dangerous. We memorialize the well-known murders of South African black consciousness activist Stephen Biko and rubber tapper and environmentalist Chico Mendes, yet people in this movement are killed and intimidated every day. When you see images of Amazon Indians marching in full regalia in São Paulo to protest Brazilian government policies, they are individuals who are as courageous as they are terrified. I have a photograph of a small Mayan girl holding her mother's hand and looking up in wide-eyed disbelief at a phalanx of black polycarbonate shields and masked police gripping their batons in Guatemala. When the members of the Revolutionary Association of the Women of Afghanistan march for women's rights without their burqas, they display an extraordinary valor, because they *know* there will be reprisals. When the Wild Yak Brigade was formed in Zhidou, China, to protect the endangered Tibetan antelope, poachers murdered its first two leaders. Most movement activists start like Chico Mendes, believing they are fighting for a specific cause—in his case rubber trees—and realize later they are fighting for a greater purpose: " . . . then I thought I was trying to save the Amazon rainforest. Now I realize I was fighting for humanity."

To deal with the pathogens, the movement has had to become an array of different types of organizations. There are institutes, community development agencies, village- and citizen-based groups, corporations, research institutes, associations, networks, faith-based groups, trusts, and foundations. Within each of these categories are dozens of types of organizations defined by their activity; within these different activities, groups have a specific focus: rights of children, cultural diversity, coral reef conservation, democratic reform, energy security, literacy, and so on.

Can myriad organizations work together to address deeper systemic issues? Do organizations step back and see where there is overlap? Do they operate efficiently? Do they try to create synergies, maximize funding, encourage efficiencies, and sublimate their identities to a larger whole? Not as much as is possible, and is necessary. But the fact that the movement is made up of pieces does not mean it can only work piecemeal.

Some would argue that it is counterproductive to conflate all the different organizations and types of organizations into a single movement, that it is self-evident that such divergent aims cannot create an effective, unified body. It's true that pluralism, the de facto tactic of a million small organizations, functions best in a society that cultivates diversity, dialogue, and collaboration. In a you-are-either-with-us-or-against-us society, small, single-issue organizations are effectively marginalized. In the United States, the environmental and social justice movements emerged in what was then a pluralistic society. Because increasingly these movements do not emerge from pluralistic societies, the stratagems and goals of the movement may be inadequate to the increasing centralization of power.

Nevertheless, if anything can offer us hope for the future, it will be an assembly of humanity that is representative but not centralized, because an ideology can never heal the wounds of this world. History demonstrates all too eloquently that no ideology has ever amounted to more than a palliative for any dire condition. The immune system is the most complex system in the body, just as the body is the most complex organism on Earth, and the most complicated assembly of organisms is human civilization.

I have friends who would vigorously protest the potential of this movement, pointing out the small-mindedness, competition, and selfishness of some NGOs and the people who lead them. But this is not a question of whether the human condition permeates the movement. It does most surely; clay feet march in all protests. It is a question of whether the underlying values of the movement are permeating global society. And there is a larger issue, the question of intent. What is the intention of the movement? If you look at the values, missions, goals, and principles of the movement, and I urge you to do so, you will see that at the core of all organizations are two principles, albeit unstated: first is the Golden Rule; second is the sacredness of all life, whether it be a creature, child, or culture. The prophets we now enshrine were ridiculed in their day. Amos was constantly in trouble with the authorities. Jeremiah became the root of the word jeremiad, which means a list of woes, but like Cassandra, he was right. David Suzuki has been right for forty years. Donella Meadows was right about biological limits to growth and was scorned by fellow scientists. Bill McKibben has been unwavering and unerring in his cautions about climate change. Martin Luther King was killed one year after he delivered his *Beyond Vietnam* address opposing the Vietnam War, berating the American military for "taking the young black men who have been crippled by our society and sending them 8,000 miles away to guarantee liberties in Southeast Asia which they had not found in southwest Georgia and East Harlem." Although she has a beautiful home in England, Jane Goodall travels three hundred days a year on behalf of the Earth, speaking, teaching, supporting, and urging others to act. Wangari Maathai was denounced in Parliament, publicly mocked for divorcing her husband, and beaten unconscious for her work on behalf of women and the African environment. It matters not how these six and other leaders will be seen in the future; for now, they are teachers

72

who try or have tried to address the suffering they witness on earth.

I once watched a large demonstration while waiting to join up with a friend. Tens of thousands of people carrying a variety of handmade placards strolled down a wide boulevard accompanied by chants, slogans, and song. The signs referred to politicians, different species, prisoners of conscience, corporate campaigns, wars, agriculture, water, workers' rights, dissidents, and more. Standing near me, a policeman was trying to understand what appeared to be a political Tower of Babel. The broad-shouldered Irishman shook his head and asked rhetorically, "What do these people want?" Fair question.

There are two kinds of games—games that end and games that don't. The rules are fixed and rigid in the first game. In the second the rules change whenever necessary to keep the game going. James Carse called these finite and infinite games. We play finite games to compete and win. They always have losers and are called business, banking, CEO, war, NBA, president, Wall Street, and politics. We play infinite games to play; they have no losers because the object of the game is to keep playing. Infinite games pay it forward and fill future coffers. They are called potlatch, family, samba, prayer, culture, tree planting, storytelling, and gospel singing.

Sustainability, ensuring the future of life on Earth, is an infinite game, the endless undertaking of generosity on behalf of all. Any action that threatens sustainability can end the game, which is why groups dedicated to keeping the game going address any harmful policy, law, or endeavor. With no invitation, they invade and permeate the finite games of the world, not to win but to change finite games into infinite games. They want to keep the fish game going, so they go after polluters of rivers. They want to keep the culture game going, so they confront oil exploration in Ecuador. They want to keep the hope game alive in the world, so they go after the roots of poverty. They want to keep the species game happening, so they buy swaths of habitat and undeveloped land. They want to keep the child game going, so when the United States violated the Geneva Conventions and bombed the 1,400 Iraqi water and sewage treatment plants in the first Gulf War, resulting in sewage, cholera, and typhus-laden water, it was morally wrong. When the same country that dropped the bombs persuaded the UN to prevent shipments of chlorine and medicine to treat the subsequent diseases, the infinite-game players thought it was a hideous thing to do and traveled to the heart of that dark, evil dictatorship to start NGOs to serve the unserved. People trying to keep the game going are activists, conservationists, biophiles, nuns, immigrants, outsiders, puppeteers, protesters, Christians, biologists, permaculturists, refugees, green architects, doctors without borders, engineers without borders, reformers, healers, poets, environmental educators, organic farmers, Buddhists, rainwater harvesters, meddlers, meditators, mediators, agitators, schoolchildren, ecofeminists, biomimics, Muslims, and social entrepreneurs.

David James Duncan penned a response to the hostile takeover of Christianity by fundamentalists, which applies to all fundamentalism: the people of the world do not need fanatic religious fundamentalists or oleaginous free-trade hucksters to save them; these people need us for their salvation, and *us* stands for the crazy-quilt assemblage of global humanity that is willing to stand up to the raw, cancerous insults that come from the mouths, guns, checkbooks, and policies of ideologues, because the movement is not merely trying to prevent wrongs but actively seeks to love this world. Compassion and love of others are at the heart of all religions and at the heart of this movement. Duncan wrote: "When small things are done with love it's not a flawed you or me who does them: it's love. I have no faith in any political party, left, right, or centrist. I have boundless faith in love. In keeping with this faith, the only spiritually responsible way I know to be a citizen, artist, or activist in these strange times is by giving little or no thought to 'great things' such as saving the planet, achieving world peace, or stopping neocon greed. Great things tend to be undoable things. Whereas small things, lovingly done, are always within our reach." Some people think the movement is defined by what it is against, but the language of the movement is about keeping the conversation going, because ideas that inform it never end: growth without inequality, wealth without plunder, work without exploitation, a future without fear. To answer the policeman's question, "these people" are reimagining the world.

THREE SHIPS

Sherilyn MacGregor

Your e-mail got buried in about 2,056 spam messages in the inbox of an account I no longer access. It is a miracle I found it, really. You sent it three months ago, which is a long time for it to have gone without a reply. I suppose if it had been lost in cyberspace, you would have written to someone else who might have sent an entirely different response, one more eloquent than mine. But there it was sandwiched between an ad for Viagra and a plea for cash from Mr B. Fayher of Lagos, Nigeria; there it was with its curious subject line ["RE: Suzuki book"] and its remarkable request for an essay "about the beauty and wonders of the ecosystem and its creatures, the severe and urgent threats they face, and some suggestions and solutions

*for countering these threats." Not the kind of request
I receive every day, or the kind that I am inclined to
leave unanswered. Doomed to failure, maybe, but I've
decided to make an attempt.*

NOT ALL READERS WILL GET THIS REFERENCE TO *Three Guineas*, published in 1938. It opens something like this, with Virginia Woolf's apology for taking so long to reply to a request to give her opinion—as a woman—about the most pressing question of her time: "How are we to prevent war?" I was reminded of her reply when I read the invitation to contribute a piece to this collection.

Three Guineas is not one of Woolf's best-known writings and was met with great scorn for its controversial feminist claims. Her answer to the question was that if women had equal access to education and professional careers, society would be transformed and there would be no more war. A similar argument is made today by many writers and activists who claim that women have special wisdom about how to solve the ecological crisis. And it seems the idea that women hold the answer to complex global problems is not so controversial anymore, at least not among environmentalists. I often get asked for my "woman's opinion" on environmental matters.

77

While writing this piece, for example, I received a request from an online magazine to comment on women's "distinct and significant contribution in protecting our natural world." What am I to say?

My work has involved researching and writing about the connections between gender, democratic politics, and the environmental crisis. My contribution is to advise caution when listening to arguments about women's unique green perspective, because I suspect it is a trap that will do neither women nor societies facing ecological collapse much good. As the feminist author Monique Wittig wrote in *The Straight Mind and Other Essays*, we should be careful not to get "entrapped in the familiar deadlock of 'woman is wonderful.' " This is not a post- or anti-feminist position, simply one that finds scant hope in the notion that femaleness alone is tantamount to being able to fix whatever it is that men have broken.

I want to make a case for moving away from the tired trap of women's special insight and for considering instead three routes through which everyone concerned about the environment might contribute to the essentially political struggle we face. I do not believe that it will be the sensibilities of women that will get us out of this mess but rather the thoughtful practice—by as many people as possible—of three "ships": citizenship, leadership, and scholarship. These practices, so central to democracy and public life, were embraced by Woolf, too, and it is for this reason that her writing resonates with me. My discussion of these three ships here is especially fitting, since David Suzuki has sailed admirably in each one of them for as long as I can remember.

Woolf wrote her epistolary essay to condemn the destruction of life caused by war and to rage against the

78

masculine values and causes of war, namely, imperialism and patriotism. Writing during the Spanish Civil War, the rise of Nazism in Germany, and the first wave of feminism in England, she offered some strongly worded arguments about the connections between women's inequality and war. Women had no responsibility for war, she argued, because they did not go to university, were excluded from the military, and could not participate fully as equal citizens in the political arena. Women should not even be asked how to prevent war, because their pacifist and sensible dispositions (whether "innate or accidental") make violence and fascism unintelligible to them. "Scarcely a human being in the course of history has fallen to a woman's rifle; the vast majority of birds and beasts have been killed by you, not by us; and it is difficult to judge what we do not share," she wrote. So in answer to the question "How are we to prevent war?" Woolf gave her "woman's opinion" that transformation to a peaceful society would come about through the education of women and the entry of women into the professions. By the end of the book, she had pledged to donate three guineas to the cause.

Seventy years later, in the first decade of the twenty-first century, it is interesting to read *Three Guineas* and replace the word "war" with the words "global warming" or "ecological crisis." Woolf's generation could not have fathomed the extent of the destruction humans would cause or the idea that war might be replaced by climate change as the most pressing global problem. This is not to say that war is no longer a serious problem—it undoubtedly is (we have Iraq, Darfur, Palestine, Chechnya, Lebanon, Afghanistan, and counting)—or that the connections between war and ecological destruction are insignificant. Nor can we say that the other pressing problem identified by Woolf, the inequality of women, has been adequately addressed. Women globally still earn less than men on average, still face sexism at work and violence in their homes, and in some places still have to fight for their education. It continues to be true that men wage wars and that some gain great power and wealth in the process. Few women, with some notable exceptions, are involved as intimately or benefit as directly as men in the waging or supporting of wars. And it is true that women for the most part are not implicated in running the resource- and waste-intensive industries that deplete and contaminate the ecosystems in every part of the globe. So when it comes to our most pressing question—*how are we to prevent the destruction of the biosphere?*—should we continue to look to women for answers?

The connection Woolf made between feminism and pacifism are today often made between feminism and environmentalism. There are women in the environmental movement who believe that women have different, more Earth-friendly values than men. Many claim that women are more concerned about the environment than men, take more responsibility for its protection and cleanup than men, and hold the special wisdom it takes to live more lightly on the Earth. These qualities are said to stem from their roles as mothers and caregivers who tend to the health and well-being of children, other loved ones, and gardens everywhere. In the 1970s ecofeminist Françoise d'Eaubonne argued that women not only are more morally outraged than men by the scale of environmental destruction but, because they give birth to new generations, also are more aware of what needs to be done to ensure a future world for them to inhabit. She was convinced that the planet placed in the hands of women would flourish for all. More recently, at an international conference on peace and globalization, Vandana Shiva has argued that women have a special role as "guardians of life and the future."

It is important to acknowledge, however, that here in the affluent "minority world" (where the principal causes of ecological crises lie), Woolf's demand for women's access to education and the professions has had a significant response. The majority of university students in Canada and the United States and in many other countries in the developed world are now women. Education has allowed most women to improve their status and to participate in all aspects of social life. While glass ceilings are a reality and the effects of gender stereotypes persist, few professions remain closed to women. There is no denying the political influence some women have had as prime ministers, chancellors, foreign secretaries, governors-general, UN Human Rights commissioners, and so on. In addition to direct roles in industry, politics, and the armed forces, women continue to be complicit in maintaining the status quo in their roles as consumers,

81

taxpayers, and voters. So are privileged women like me innocent bystanders who can still claim not to be responsible? Or could it be argued that seventy years of social and political change have given women equal opportunities to destroy the planet? Have we in effect won and taken up equal opportunities to produce and consume, to enjoy convenience products, labor-saving technologies, unrestricted global travel, and unlimited self-indulgent luxuries? Maybe it is time to acknowledge that our education and professional careers have allowed us to join men in the pursuit of wealth through ecologically destructive means. As environmental educator David Orr has memorably (if facetiously) asked, in his book *Ecological Literacy,* what is education for these days if not to ensure one's purchasing power?

It seems counterproductive to sustain the myth that women are innately more peaceful and ecologically responsible than men. Opinion surveys have yielded contradictory findings over the years, and even when studies have found slight gender differences in environmental attitudes and behavior, it would be unfair to suggest that all women care more and do more than all men. Not only does this suggestion deny the evidence that women are also often times complicit in environmental degradation, but it also plays into assumptions that women *should* be the ones to clean up after the party. This assumption simply expands an old domestic tradition to a global scale. And, of course, there are countless examples of men who participate actively and are leaders in all aspects of environmentalism.

Iris Murdoch was critical of Woolf's habit of drawing a distinction between women's private sensibilities and men's public intellect (especially because Woolf herself was no "angel in the house"). Murdoch argued that the contributions of women to politics would be advanced more by erasing these distinctions than by affirming them. The danger of claiming women's innate superiority is that we merely occupy a self-congratulatory (perhaps self-sacrificing) niche on the sidelines and fail to cultivate the ways of thinking and acting that are evidently lacking—yet urgently needed—in both women and men. It is unfortunate that Woolf's arguments about female superiority have overshadowed her own exemplary practice of generic public virtues. If she were writing today, I think she would agree that we need to cultivate the virtues of good citizenship, leadership, and scholarship if women are to participate effectively in public debates about environmental issues. These three ships are, in my view, the keys to finding constructive and democratic answers to our twenty-first-century political and ecological questions.

83

CITIZENSHIP

"Environmental citizenship" is an important new concept on the political stage. The term was coined by the Canadian government in the early 1990s, around the time of the Rio Earth Summit. It has since become a topic of interest among environmental scholars and activists, who want as many people as possible to participate in debates about sustainability. They generally define environmental citizenship as including rights to a liveable and sustainable environment and a responsibility to be informed, to participate actively in decision making, and to protect and restore ecosystem health for present and future generations. To be a good environmental citizen is to have a sense of connectedness to place (be it a country or a bioregion) and feelings of solidarity and compassion for those in other parts of the world who are paying (or will pay) the price of our privilege. Environmental citizenship includes a commitment to democracy and the common ecological good, active participation in public deliberation, involvement in one's community, and political, economic, and scientific literacy. I emphasize citizenship in my work because, along with many other environmental scholars, I believe that the ecological crisis is a political and social crisis. If this is so, we must look not only to science and technology for solutions but also to the ways in which we organize and sustain ourselves collectively.

I have written elsewhere that citizenship is a more appropriate language through which to express environmental concerns than the depoliticizing language of care. The tendency among some environmentalists and ecofeminists to use private sentiments to express political arguments (as in "we need to care for the Earth" or

84

"it's time for women to mother Earth") is dangerous in an era when citizenship and public-mindedness are under threat from the same ideological forces that threaten the planet. Woolf's generation was struggling for the right to practice political citizenship, yet my generation seems to have forgotten that it means so much more than casting a vote or applying for a passport. This amnesia is partly due, I think, to the rise of neoliberalism, a pernicious ideology that pushes privatization, commercialization, and the creation of a global economy in which space, place, and time are increasingly irrelevant. Neoliberalism has successfully perpetuated the myth that we are individual consumers, investors, homeowners, and taxpayers rather than citizens with shared interests. As we become increasingly obsessed with our private lives (and those of celebrities), we lose sight of the fact that the quality of our private lives depends on the quality of our public spaces and institutions. In this climate we need to cultivate and defend the concept of citizenship more than ever—and to make its practice an essential part of the environmental agenda.

LEADERSHIP

Environmental citizenship is important, but we can't expect citizens to do it all. Nor should they shoulder the bulk of the blame. I often hear environmentalists say that we need to educate people to behave more eco-responsibly. Education is undoubtedly important, but

85

it is dangerous to assume that people fail to act out of ignorance when there are major structural causes of our ecological unsustainability. Changing these structural (i.e., social, economic, and political) causes depends on leadership, which brings me to the idea that leadership is as important as citizenship.

In addition to "doing their bit," citizens should also ask: What are the leaders doing? Whose interests do they serve? Who makes the decision to take a country to war or build new nuclear power stations or opt out of the Kyoto Protocol? Who steers corporations in the direction of the cheapest possible resources while externalizing the ecological costs of doing business? Who has the power to make and enforce the policies, regulations, and laws that are so desperately needed?

Most of our current leaders will need to be educated (i.e., deprogrammed, then retrained) while we develop new kinds of environmental leadership for the future. We need leaders who will take risks, make demands, listen, and respond to public expertise. Leaders can also be thought of as exemplary citizens who motivate and inspire others and make collective projects happen. Elected politicians can be one kind of environmental leader, but it is a fact of our democratic system that politicians have a planning horizon that is entirely at odds with ecological processes. Community organizers and elders are especially influential leaders. There are many grassroots initiatives around the world that are led by exceptional women and men who choose to determine the direction of environmental change rather than go with the flow.

A citizen's role is to hold elected leaders to account and to demand that they serve the public good. We need more opportunities to do so. One example to celebrate is the David Suzuki Foundation's 2007 "If you were Prime Minister" cross-country tour, which asked tens of thousands of Canadians to debate their environmental priorities and express their opinions to decision makers. The tour's recommendations affirm that citizens want environmental rights as well as more responsibilities. They want politicians to regulate corporate activities rather than keep markets open for unfettered business. The tour put citizens into dialogue with each other, and citizens into dialogue with their leaders, who should now be compelled to act. It undoubtedly created a leader or two in each community along the way.

SCHOLARSHIP

The American philosopher John Dewey (also writing seventy years ago) believed that the development of a healthy democratic culture depends on the artful communication of intellectual insights to resist debilitating orthodoxies and to bolster public deliberation. Virginia Woolf was herself an engaged scholar who spoke out on the issues of her day, as *Three Guineas* exemplifies. She once explained her desire to publicize her opinions about war and fascism by saying that "thinking is my fighting." Scholars

87

and public intellectuals have a particularly valuable role to play in fighting global ecological problems and neoliberalism at this moment in history.

If we are ever to answer the question—*how are we to prevent the destruction of the biosphere?*—the role of environmental scholars who can make their critical insights accessible through their teaching, writing, and research should not be underestimated. We need scholars who are permanently curious, never closing down the search for answers by claiming to know the final word. Scientists have done as much harm as good where the planet is concerned (and where women are concerned) by dominating the conversation and failing to listen to their objects of study. They do us all a much greater service when they reflect critically on the commitments and assumptions that underpin their research questions and publicly contest the myth that it is up to science to produce certainties before action can be rationally justified.

The world is full of competing views of nature and humanity's place in nature, held by different intellectual traditions and belief systems. Increasing the number of participants in producing knowledge, and the intensity of dialogue between them, increases the chance that useful insight and social change will emerge. Perhaps we need to recognize that knowledge-diversity (like biodiversity) can only flourish in a healthy democratic environment. Public intellectuals can contribute to this democratizing project by making scientific knowledge about nature accessible and intelligible to as many citizens and leaders as possible.

The life of a scholar is not for everyone, and scholarship is commonly seen (rightly or wrongly) to be elitist and removed from the so-called real world. Scholarship is admittedly not as big as my two other ships, but it is nevertheless important to value the countless environmental scholars in a range of disciplines who are devoted to serving the public and promoting the common good. David Suzuki is one of them. He has done a remarkable job of teaching us about the nature of things, while being passionately open to debate and never being shy about making political arguments. I like to think of him as a free-range citizen-scholar who knows how to lead. People who are good leaders, scholars, and citizens all rolled into one, with generous sprinklings of humility and humor, are from a rare and endangered species.

CONFESSIONS OF A FORMER ENVIRONMENTAL SKEPTIC

Michael Shermer

IN HIS 1964 SPEECH ACCEPTING THE REPUBLICAN presidential nomination, Barry Goldwater delivered one of the most memorable one-liners in political punditry: "Extremism in the defense of liberty is no vice. Moderation in the pursuit of justice is no virtue."

These are stirring sentiments, to be sure, and once in a great while they may even be true. But for most human endeavors, moderation is a virtue and extremism is a vice. The reason is clear: all extremists—from Torquemada and Timothy McVeigh to abortion clinic bombers and the 9/11 terrorists—think they are defending liberty and pursuing justice. One country's terrorist is another country's freedom fighter.

Extreme environmentalists are a case in point. Members of environmentalist groups who vandalize Hummer dealerships, destroy logging equipment, or torch scientific laboratories see themselves not as the terrorists that they are but as environmental freedom fighters. And environmental groups who paint doom-and-gloom scenarios and exaggerate, distort, or even fabricate claims to keep the donations flowing only hurt their cause in the long run when doomsday comes and goes without incident.

As an undergraduate in the early 1970s, I was told that overpopulation would lead to worldwide hunger and starvation, oil depletion, exhaustion of precious minerals, and extinction of the rain forest by the 1990s, predictions that have all failed utterly to come true. Scientists like Bjorn Lomborg in his book *The Skeptical Environmentalist's Guide to Global Warming* have, in my opinion, properly nailed environmental extremists for these exaggerated scenarios. And his book is where I entered the debate.

In 2001 Cambridge University Press published Lomborg's book, which, given the similarity between its title and that of the magazine that I publish (*Skeptic*), his publicist thought would be a perfect topic for the Skeptics Society's public science lecture series at the California Institute of Technology, which I host. Because of the highly debatable nature of many of Lomborg's claims, however, I only agreed to invite him if the event could be a debate. Lomborg accepted at once, and this is where the trouble began—I could not find anyone to debate him.

I contacted all of the top environmental organizations, and to a one they refused to participate. "There is no debate," one told me. "We don't want to dignify that book," said another. One leading environmentalist warned me that my reputation would be irreparably harmed if I went through with it. So of course I did. Finally, my own senior editor, Frank Miele, who is an expert on evolutionary biology and biodiversity (and is one of the fastest and most facile researchers I've ever known), challenged Lomborg on several of the chapters in his book, and we had a lively and successful debate.

My experience is symptomatic of deep problems that have long plagued the environmental movement, and for a time the political pollution of the science turned me into an environmental skeptic. That alone would be meaningless, since I have only ever written one article on the subject, but I believe that the extremists had a similar effect on millions of others who remain skeptical in the teeth of what I now believe to be overwhelming evidence for anthropogenic—that is, influenced by human beings—global warming. The tragedy of this inappropriate conflation of politics and science is that although world-class scientists and science communicators like David Suzuki have been warning us about this problem for decades in a systematic and reasonable manner, many of us failed to hear the warnings because of the extremists' claims.

What turned me around on the global warming issue was a convergence of evidence from numerous sources. My interest was piqued on February 8, 2006, when eighty-six leading evangelical Christians—the last cohort I expected to get on the environmental bandwagon—issued the Evangelical Climate Initiative calling for "national legislation requiring economy-wide reductions" in carbon emissions. After attending a 2002 conference in Oxford on the science of global warming, the chief lobbyist for the National Association of Evangelicals, the Reverend Richard Cizik, described his experience as "a conversion... not unlike my conversion to Christ."

Later that month I attended the TED (Technology, Entertainment, Design) conference in Monterey, California, where former Vice President Al Gore delivered the finest summation of the evidence for global warming I have ever heard, based on the 2006 documentary film about his work in this area, *An Inconvenient Truth*. Because we are primates with visually dominant sensory systems, we need to *see* the evidence to believe it, and the striking visuals of countless graphs and charts, and especially the before-and-after photographs showing the disappearance of glaciers around the world, shocked me viscerally and knocked me out my skepticism.

Four recent books on the subject then took me to the flipping point. Archaeologist Brïan Fagan's *The Long Summer* documents how civilization is the gift of a temporary period of mild climate. Geographer Jared Diamond's *Collapse* demonstrates how natural and human-caused environmental catastrophes led to the collapse of civilizations. Journalist Elizabeth Kolbert's *Field Notes From a Catastrophe* is a page-turning account of her journeys around the world with environmental scientists who are documenting species extinction and climate change that are unmistakably linked to human action. And biologist

Tim Flannery's *The Weather Makers* reveals how he went from being a skeptical environmentalist to a believing activist as incontrovertible data linking the increase of carbon dioxide to global warming accumulated over the last decade.

It is a matter of carbon dioxide, Goldilocks. In the last ice age, carbon dioxide levels were 180 parts per million (ppm)—too cold. Between the agricultural revolution and the industrial revolution, carbon dioxide levels rose to 280 ppm—just right. Today carbon dioxide levels are at 380 ppm and are projected to reach 450 to 550 ppm by the end of the century—too warm. Like a kettle of water that transforms from liquid to steam when it changes from 211 to 212 degrees Fahrenheit, the environment itself is about to make a carbon dioxide–driven flip.

According to Flannery, even if we reduce our carbon dioxide emissions by 70 percent by 2050, average global temperatures will increase between two to nine degrees Celsius by 2100. This rise could lead to the melting of the Greenland Ice Sheet, which the March 24, 2007, issue of *Science* reports is already shrinking at a rate of 224 ±41 cubic kilometers per year, double the rate measured in 1996 (for comparison, Los Angeles uses 1 cubic kilometer of water per year). If it and the West Antarctic Ice Sheet melt, sea levels will rise five to ten meters, displacing half a billion inhabitants of coastal communities.

The only article I ever wrote about the environment, published in my monthly column in *Scientific American,* recounted my conversion from global warming skeptic to believer. In that column I closed with these sentences: "Because of the complexity of the problem, environmental skepticism was once tenable. No longer. It is time to flip from skepticism to activism."

What I meant is that it is time to do something about the problem. I did not specify what we should do, but in my opinion we have time to fix the problem without drastic and draconian governmental intervention. As one example, I believe that if we start the transition now, we can make the shift from burning fossil fuels to using alternative fuels through normal market channels. The market for hybrid automobiles, for instance, will continue growing at a breakneck pace such that within two decades the vast majority of cars will be hybrids and we will make the transition to purely electric cars (or cars that run on some other combination of electricity and a cleaner alternative fuel). If governments establish pollution standards and carbon dioxide levels, the marketplace can then work around them efficiently—more efficiently, in any case, than most government programs can.

In response to my *Scientific American* column, I received thousands of letters and e-mails. A few were surprised that it took me so long to come around:

Well, gosh, Shermer, welcome to the party. Where the heck have you been? No offense, but most of your readers realized it was "time to flip" years ago . . . If

it took four books and a lecture by Al Gore to change
your mind, I despair that we will ever change the
minds of the people who really matter: the voters.
—BH, California

Indeed, my correspondent is right. The bulk of letters that I received were skeptical of my loss of skepticism. In spite of what I now see as overwhelming evidence for anthropogenic global warming, there are still plenty of skeptics out there, and I believe that like me they got burned by environmental extremists. Here is a small sampling.

Michael Shermer sure has "flipped!" He quotes Flan-
nery as saying that "even if we reduce our carbon dioxide
emissions by seventy percent by 2050, average global
temperatures will increase between two and nine degrees
by 2050." Could it be that global warming is caused, in
the main, by forces beyond our control?—RS, California

I was disappointed to see that Mr. Shermer has surren-
dered his skepticism on anthropogenic global warming.
His "flipping point" seems to be the demonstrated reduc-
tion in some of the world's glaciers. I suggest he enroll in a
freshman course in historical geology . . . I think his change
of heart will turn out to be as wrong as his stated belief in
the 1970s that starvation and depletion of resources would
plague the earth by the 1990s.—HS, Colorado

You have joined the philistines. The blunt, highlighted in red, comment: "Reducing our CO_2 emissions by seventy percent by 2050 will not be enough" shows a grab at a statement that would put even the most rabid environmental group to shame. Prove it!—ID, Ontario

MY RESPONSE TO these and the many other letters I received about this issue is similar to my reply to creationists who point out that this or that anomaly that doesn't fit the prevailing paradigm. That is, evolution, like global climate change, is not "proved" through this or that fact, which if debunked would send the whole theoretical ship to the ocean floor. Instead, we have a vast convergence of evidence from multiple lines of scientific inquiry, all of which independently but in tandem point to the conclusion that global warming is real, most likely human caused, and is something we need to think seriously about in our political and economic responses.

I well remember watching television programs about the environment hosted by David Suzuki. They were visually stunning and brilliantly presented. But my mind had already been hardened by the failed predictions of the extremists, and so I watched and listened, but I did not see or hear. But you were right, David, and for many decades of tireless work on behalf of this pale blue dot and its inhabitants, we all owe you a debt of gratitude.

THE MECHANICAL SAVIOR:
NATURE AND THE ILLUSION OF TECHNOLOGY

—— *Wayne Grady* ——

IN THE WAKE OF KATRINA'S DESTRUCTION OF NEW Orleans in September 2005, President George W. Bush was quick to announce that the United States was about to experience gasoline shortages, and therefore higher fuel prices, because the hurricane had severed pipelines between the Louisiana coast and drilling rigs in the Gulf of Mexico. He even urged Americans to use less gasoline, at least temporarily. Eventually, he said, "technology will find a solution." Technology would find a way to get the oil flowing again.

A year later, when Prime Minister Stephen Harper announced his minority government's Clean Air Bill, he mentioned that technological improvements would ultimately reduce total carbon dioxide emissions by 60 percent by the year 2050. "With technological change," he said, "massive reductions in emissions are possible. We have reason to believe that by harnessing technology we can make large-scale reductions." Again, technology would find a way. Technology would save us.

Both Bush and Harper are deeply religious men. It seems to me that belief in God and belief in technology have become very closely related. Technology has come to be a form of redemption: Bush and Harper both state that someone or something will come along to save us from our own excesses. That is a fundamentally religious belief. In a former age, they would have said that God would find a way. Now they say technology will.

The link between religion and technology is not a new one: it was forged between the ninth and the twelfth centuries, with the invention of such earth-altering devices as the heavy plow, the waterwheel, and the windmill, when technology was called "the mechanical arts." There had been mechanical devices long before that, of course, but as David F. Noble remarks in *The Religion of Technology,* these new mechanical inventions changed humankind's relationship with the physical world; they allowed us to move from being a mere "part of nature" to becoming "exploiters of nature." With the ability to improve the natural world on a grand scale, not only were human beings imitating God, they were able to complete God's creation of the universe (or to at least allow God to complete His work through them), to make the world closer to "perfect." Also, by means of the mechanical arts humans could

99

restore the Earth to its prelapsarian splendor: we could reverse the Fall of Man and return to Eden.

What is new to this century, I believe, is the exalted status George Bush and Stephen Harper bestow on what is, essentially, a tool. Historically, technology was an aid in fulfilling humankind's purpose on Earth, which was to redeem ourselves from Original Sin and thereby become more Godlike. Now, however, technology seems to have become more Godlike itself. If by the sixteenth century technology had eroded the distinction between Man and God, making both creators of the physical environment, in the twenty-first century it is the distinction between God and technology that has become blurred. Now technology is the creator, as well as the savior, of humankind.

Call me a Luddite, but wasn't it technology that got us into this environmental fix in the first place? Relying on technology to solve problems created by an overweening reliance on technology smacks to me of aversion therapy.

BEING CALLED A Luddite these days is a kind of automatic put-down, the implication being that one is too stupid or clumsy to figure out how to drive a car with standard transmission or download a five-megabyte pdf file without losing it to the ether. The kind of person who thinks dial-up is plenty fast enough, thank you, or who looks blank when told by a mechanic that his timing belt needs replacing. Preferring to lessen the impact of technological innovation on our personal lives is seen not as a considered option but rather as an admission of our innate inability to comprehend how the world works. C.P. Snow used the term in 1959 in his famous Rede Lecture, "The Two Cultures and the Scientific Revolution," in which he referred to intellectuals of the "literary faction" as "natural Luddites," people who had "never tried, wanted or been able to understand" the significance of the Industrial Revolution. It used to be the other way around. The original Luddites understood the significance of the Industrial Revolution all too well. In 1779 a Leicestershire mill worker named Ned Ludd broke into a factory at night and smashed two machines used to knit stockings. He acted, reportedly, "in a fit of insane rage," and Luddism has been associated with insanity or worse ever since. But Ludd was acting from a clear vision of what technology was going to do to the working classes. English mill owners had begun importing knitting frames from Germany that allowed them to produce hosiery and lace with fewer human hands, and consequently thousands of English textile workers like Ned Ludd had been thrown out of work. Ludd became a folk hero among mill workers, especially in Yorkshire, where, in 1811, bands of hooded men began breaking into woolen mills, smashing machinery, and burning bales of cloth. They abstained from bloodshed, but in 1812 several frame breakers were shot down by soldiers called in by a mill owner, who was subsequently found murdered. After a trial in 1813, many convicted Luddites, possibly including Ned Ludd, were hanged or transported to Australia.

One early member of Snow's "literary faction" was Charlotte Brontë, whose three-volume novel *Shirley* takes place in Yorkshire during the Luddite disturbances. Brontë had grown up in Luddite country—her father was a Yorkshire clergyman, a friend of a local mill owner, and an outspoken opponent of Luddite violence. She presents both sides of the dispute, however, depicting the plight both of the starving mill workers and of the desperate owners and merchants who, because of Napoleon's blockade, had been unable to sell their textiles abroad for several years and needed the machinery to lower production costs for the domestic market. Yes, there were many people out of work at the mills, but a great many of them were children. The ethics of the situation were, as always, somewhat murky. Brontë seems to have believed that the best thing for everyone would be for the war with Napoleon to end and for things to get back to normal.

Before Brontë, Lord Byron's inaugural speech in the House of Lords, delivered at the height of the Luddite troubles, was sympathetic to the plight of the workers but also conscious of the difficulties faced by the merchants: "Had the grievances of these men and their masters (for they also had their grievances) been fairly weighed and justly examined," he declaimed, "I do think that means might have been devised to restore these workmen to their avocations, and tranquility to the country." But Byron was

speaking against the bill that would make frame breaking a hanging offense, and five years later, when another
eruption of Luddism took place, Byron wrote "Song of
the Luddites," (1816) a stirring call to arms that showed
where his true sympathies lay:

> As the Liberty lads o'er the sea
> Bought their freedom, and cheaply, with blood,
> So we, boys, we
> Will die fighting, or live free,
> And down with all kings but King Ludd.

Although he doesn't mention Luddism, Samuel Butler
explored the rejection of technology in the utopian novel
Erewhon, published in 1872. His narrator, Higgs, stumbles
across a remote society in New Zealand that has turned
back time by outlawing every mechanical advancement
made in Europe during the previous five hundred years.
The Erewhonians had spoons, shovels, horse-drawn
carts, and even fine textiles but no machines, no trains or
steam-driven knitting frames. Higgs is arrested and jailed
for owning a pocket watch.

Curiously, they also had no religion. Moral issues were
settled not by priests but by philosophers. The Erewhonians were not simple or bumbling savages; they were
intelligent, civilized, cultured, and content. Erewhon was
like England might have been had the Luddites won the
day in 1811. Perhaps Butler was inspired in part by Marx's

Das Kapital, which had appeared in 1867 and included the statement that "the production of too many useful things results in too many useless people." In Erewhon the only useless person was Higgs.

Butler's vision was as farsighted as Marx's. Outside Erewhon, Butler believed, machines had taken on independent lives of their own. Humans had become slaves to machines. He even ascribed to them a degree of intelligence—"Who can say that the vapour machine [the steam engine] has not a kind of consciousness? Where does consciousness begin, and where end? Who can draw the line? Is not everything interwoven with everything?"—as well as the ability to reproduce themselves (using humans as midwives): "Do we not use a machine to make a new part for a machine?" Are we not making computers that are capable of thought? Honda Motors has announced that a walking, artificially intelligent android is now working as a receptionist at a Honda office near Tokyo. Researchers elsewhere say they have developed "a self-aware, curious robot that can diagnose its own problems and take concrete steps to heal itself." Are we surprised by these developments?

According to Butler, humans, like domesticated animals, have become so dependent upon the artificial environment created for us by machines that we can no longer survive without them; machines have become our "extra-corporeal limbs"; removing them would be a kind of amputation. So reliant upon technology have we become that our very survival as a species depends upon it: "If all machines were to be annihilated at one moment," he writes, "and all knowledge of mechanical laws were taken from [us] so that [we] could make no more machines, and all machine-made food destroyed so that the race of man should be left as it were naked upon a desert island, we should become extinct in six weeks."

The irrational, millennial panic that surrounded Y2K should have told us a lot about what we do when we think we are going to have our machines taken away from us, even for a few hours. We behave like heroin addicts in a detox center. We talk about "collapsing economies" and "imploding infrastructures." We have gone well beyond being dependent upon technology for our comfort and convenience; we have been domesticated by it.

John Livingston writes in *Rogue Primate* that "human domestication is, nearly enough, a synonym for civilization." Collectively, like a breed of domesticated beasts, we have accepted the benefits of civilization at the expense of our individual freedom. If we occasionally revert to primitive behavior, such as breaking into factories and smashing machines, we are characterized as "insane" and executed, transported, locked away in lunatic asylums, or forced to undergo psychiatric treatment. That, for example, is the burden of Freud's *Civilization and Its Discontents*: individually, we have brief, mental flashbacks to our precivilized selves, and the resulting discontent drives us insane.

Freud defends civilization on the grounds that it has greatly improved our physical well-being—we lead longer, healthier lives, enjoy a steadier supply of food, have adequate shelter from "the harsh effects of nature"—in short, we have accrued the same benefits that animals receive when they are domesticated. But even Freud notes that these accomplishments have been achieved at a great cost to our psychological health, in that we are constantly called upon to resolve, and alarmingly often fail to resolve, conflicts between our natural, individual desires and the communal behavior imposed upon us by society. "The word 'civilization,' " he writes, "designates the sum total of those achievements and institutions that distinguish our life from that of our animal ancestors." It thus measures the difference between wild and domesticated. He cites technology as the prime example of our "cultural acquisitions," noting that by extending our ability to control the external forces of nature, it has given us "god-like" stature: echoing Butler, he notes that thanks to technology "man has become, so to speak, a god with artificial limbs." He predicts that "distant ages will bring new and probably unimaginable advances in this field of civilization and so enhance his god-like nature. But in the interest of our investigation let us also remember that modern man does not feel happy with his god-like nature." Domesticated humans still yearn for individual freedom, and that yearning is the source of our neuroses.

Most of Freud's patients came to him, he believed, because of the conflict between their natural sexual natures and the restrictions imposed upon them by civilization. Picture Ned Ludd lying on Freud's couch trying to explain why he reaches for his sledgehammer whenever he sees a knitting frame and Freud trying to integrate him back into domesticity. Freud's patients wanted the freedom to mate at will with any preferred partners, including family members (as many wild primates do), but felt prevented from doing so by invented social mores. The resulting psychic split made them hysterical. Generalizing this split, Freud writes that "much of mankind's struggle is taken up with the task of finding a suitable, that is to say a happy, accommodation between the claims of the individual and the mass claims of civilization." A successful accommodation, however, involves such high levels of sublimation and the suppression of our most powerful libidinal drives that the effort to achieve it causes huge psychic damage. We recognize the need for the leash, but we strain against it. Accommodating to civilization "cannot be done without risk," Freud writes. "One can expect serious disturbances."

THE LUDDITES PRODUCED some serious disturbances, but they caused hardly a misstep in the steady march of progress for progress's sake. In a confrontational scene in *Shirley,* one of the more reasonable frame breakers, William Farren, appeals to the proprietor of the local woolen mill, a hard-nosed merchant named Moore who might have been modeled on the mill owner who ordered the Luddites shot down in 1812.

"Ye're a raight hard un," Farren tells Moore. "Will n't ye gie us a bit o' time?—Will n't ye consent to mak' your changes rather more slowly?"

"If I stopped by the way an instant," Moore replies, "while others are rushing in, I should be trodden down. If I did as you wish me to do, I should be bankrupt in a month: and would my bankruptcy put bread into your hungry children's mouths?"

Farren's is an emotional request; but Moore's is a reasonable reply, and we are in the Age of Reason. Moore's answer to Farren is the answer all technocrats give to any plea for moderation or moral consideration. It is C.P. Snow's reply to the intellectuals. If we do not develop the atom bomb, someone else will. If we do not genetically modify corn, soybeans, canola, and wheat to resist pesticides and drought, we will not be able to feed the Earth's rapidly expanding population. If we cut back on fossil fuel consumption, the economy will collapse. Technology now proceeds at its own pace, with no regard to the walking gait of humanity—as physicist Barry Commoner has put it, "technology is now doing more than science knows"—and all the neo-Luddites are asking is for it to slow down, give us a bit more time to adjust, let us examine the ethical implications of cloning, let us ask ourselves if we want or need robots to answer our telephones or beef steaks grown from bovine stem cells or beetle-killing pine trees.

"Is there something about reading and thinking," asked novelist Thomas Pynchon in 1984 in the *New York Times,*

108

"that would cause or predispose a person to turn Luddite? Is it okay to be a Luddite?" Pynchon viewed Luddism, along with other forms of radical behavior, including novel writing, as part of "a broad front of resistance to the Age of Reason," a deep-seated reluctance "to give up elements of faith, however 'irrational,' to an emerging technopolitical order that might or might not know what it was doing."

Since 1984, and since *1984*, we have gone beyond technopolitical. What has been created is an unprecedented merger of technology and politics (which is really applied economics) and elements of faith, an extremely volatile mixture in which any ideology can be called upon to justify any kind of behaviour. The merger has produced what may be termed a cult of technology, an adherence to technology that has more to do with faith than with reason, and therefore nothing to do with science. Technology will solve all ills, be they economic, political, or environmental. To question this belief, even to examine it, is to be a heretic, a Luddite. Writing in 1939, the German economist Friedrich Juenger warned that "there can be no talk of riches produced by technology. What really happens is rather a steady, forever growing consumption." The goal of economics, Juenger wrote, is profit, whereas the goal of technology is, or ought to be, "the drive to perfection." When economics fails, he adds, writing during the Depression, the technologist takes over and creates a technocracy, "a role for which the technologist has no training or expertise." In a technocracy, technology is God, and forever growing consumption is worship.

IN 1902, A disillusioned but ever-prescient Butler wrote *Erewhon Revisited,* in which Higgs returns to Erewhon to find it immeasurably changed as a result of his own earlier visit: the Erewhonians have embraced machines, their politics have become intricately entangled with religion and art (the high priests are also managers of the Musical Bank), their economy has collapsed, and their infrastructure has imploded. The Luddites have lost and the merchants have taken over. Higgs is arrested as a raving lunatic and sentenced to death. In case we miss the analogy, Higgs escapes from Erewhon and returns to England, where he is declared a raving lunatic and placed in an asylum, where he dies.

How many warnings do we need?

BUILDING BACKWARDS

Alan Weisman ·

PAQUIMÉ WAS A WONDER WHEN IT ROSE—A MULTI-
tiered earthen city spreading across the northern Chihuahuan altiplano, built over hundreds of years by the
Casas Grandes people. Possibly Mescalero Apaches finally
sacked it, although it is more likely that rather than any
sudden calamity, protracted drought during the four-
teenth century gradually drove its residents out.

Paquimé is a wonder going down, too. The natural life
span of earthwork buildings resembles our own: a slow
upward curve, then—with luck—an even gentler descent
as weathering and gravity redistribute each stone and
bone, molecule by molecule, until only dust is left. Today
Paquimé's mud-and-wood viga roofs are long gone. As its
meter-thick walls are tugged back into the Chihuahuan
plains, their once-straight lines have smoothed into pleas-
ing tan and pink clay parabolas. Seen from afar, Paquimé

describes a naturally bell-shaped earthen timeline, a living, lovely organic relic of pre-Columbian urban glory for which the archaeological descriptor *ruin* simply misses the point.

From his new home, Nicolás Quezada can see Paquimé. He lives in Nuevo Casa Grandes, a modern Mexican example of what has happened since urban construction segued from mud to harder stuff—not stone, but the artificial kind we learned to make by adding energy to materials, not always with the intended results. Nicolás himself knows better—he is of the famous Quezada family of ceramists and potters of the town of Mata Ortiz, Chihuahua, a village on the Río Palanganas, fifteen miles southwest of Nuevo Casas Grandes' uncontrolled spill of brick and reinforced concrete. It was Nicolás's brother, Juan Quezada, who rescued a Chihuahuan technique that the earth had nearly swallowed: making eggshell pottery of surprising strength, using colors of lasting brilliance in patterns he saw in broken bits of Casas Grandes and Mimbres stoneware that, along with Paquimé, were all that remained of his altiplano's former grand and populous cultures.

As a young man gathering kindling in the hills, Juan Quezada would often find sherds of these missing cultures. He studied their composition and hunted the arroyos for deposits of the purest, most colorful clays, from which he guessed they'd been derived. Then he tried to reproduce them. In the high desert, riparian cottonwoods were too

precious to cut for fuel to fire clay, so, like his ancient pre-
decessors, Quezada used readily available animal dung.
Eventually, he learned that to forge pots that wouldn't
shatter in low-heat dung fires meant mixing pure clays
with a grog of sand and volcanic ash.

His first successful vessels, whose painted designs
departed intriguingly from Casas Grandes forms, were
discovered in 1964 by an anthropologist in a New Mexico
secondhand shop, and a modern ceramic dynasty was
born. Juan Quezada taught his ten siblings, and they all
spread his knowledge to their children and kin. Today
pots by fine Mata Ortiz ceramists are displayed in muse-
ums worldwide, and among the most coveted are those
by the Quezada family. Brother Nicolás's own work—he
was Juan's first pupil—is especially prized for his unusual
mixtures of clays, especially the fragile whites. Nicolás's
solutions to various technical problems of dung-fired
pottery helped to make Mata Ortiz the aesthetic phenomenon it has become—and that development, in turn, has
allowed him to afford his new house on the edge of the
new city.

"*¿Pero Nicolás, no está a revés?*—aren't you doing it backwards?" I asked him one early spring day in 2001. At five
thousand feet, temperatures in Chihuahua dipped below
freezing at night, and a crust of ice floated in a puddle
near the stout wall Nicolas was erecting to surround his
new three-bedroom home. "Why are you building the
wall out of adobe and the house out of brick?"

113

Quezada knew exactly what I meant. Especially in the high desert, where temperatures can fluctuate forty degrees Fahrenheit in a single day, an adobe house stays warm in the winter and cool in the blistering summer. Firing a mud brick makes it hard and durable but literally bakes the life out of the organic mass that produces its insulating values. Quezada's pointed gray beard bobbed as he nodded, pulling his fleece vest tighter. "It should be the other way around. This damn house is freezing."

So why?

"*Porque adobe no vale nada.*" Adobe is considered worthless, he explained, according to a society obsessed with upward mobility, and especially according to real estate agents.

"Mud is the material of poor people. The way you show that you've made it in the world is by having a home of solid brick. No one who can afford more wants a house of adobe, even though it would be much better. *Está loco, ¿no?*"

A FEW MONTHS later, in the neighboring northwestern Mexico state of Sonora, I saw how Nicolás's dilemma involved much more than merely a display of status. In Mexico, as in much of the populous developing world, home construction is a force that drives sweeping economic policies, with enormous implications for both the natural and social environments. As I'd seen at Nuevo Casas Grandes, in Sonora they were getting it backwards on a massive scale.

I had traveled to Ciudad Obregón, a city of about 450,000, for a look at what I hoped was truly a way to do it better. Ciudad Obregón lies in the fertile Yaqui Valley between Mexico's Sierra Madre Occidental and the coast of the Sea of Cortez. In a mountainous country where less than a fifth of the land is suitable for agriculture, sediments dropped by rivers that drain the Sierra Madre have made this one of Mexico's finest food-producing regions. Unfortunately, much of the produce is exported to the United States, in the form of winter vegetables, and—especially from Ciudad Obregón—wheat. More than a million acres planted in golden grain surround this city, known as Mexico's breadbasket and also as the birthplace of the so-called Green Revolution. In these fields, experiments from the International Maize and Wheat Improvement Center near Mexico City, which more than doubled grain yields through forced crossbreeding, were first reproduced on a massive commercial scale. Their success in world markets was multiplied many times over by makers of the fertilizers, herbicides, and pesticides needed to protect these lab-bred crops from the ravages of reality outdoors.

This engineered wheat, however, was lately being put to a promising new use: as a building material. In 1999, Jorge Valenzuela, director of the Sonoran branch of the international Save the Children foundation, had traveled to Tucson for a presentation at the University of Arizona by Bill and Athena Steen, authors of a book titled *The Straw Bale House*. Bill Steen, part Mexican, grew up in an adobe home in Arizona. He met his wife, Athena, when he visited her native village, New Mexico's Santa Clara Pueblo, to see a house she'd built from bales of straw stacked like giant bricks and plastered with mud.

Jorge Valenzuela immediately recognized what the excellent thermal properties of straw-bale architecture could mean to his city, Ciudad Obregón, where temperatures can approach 120 degrees Fahrenheit in summer and drop below freezing on winter nights. Could the Steens possibly come? "All we do is burn the wheat straw left after the harvest," he said. "Instead of sending all that carbon into the atmosphere, we could build an entire city." He proposed that they start with an office for Save the Children. It would become a model, he said, for what could be done using local straw, mud, and labor.

Bill and Athena agreed. Two years later, Save the Children-Sonora was ensconced in a five-thousand-square-foot classic Spanish courtyard structure, featuring vaulted roofs and two-foot-thick straw-bale walls, plastered in local natural clay tones ranging from ochre to cornflower blue. The building was so strikingly beautiful that it immediately became a local tourist attraction. Visitors were further impressed, a beaming Jorge Valenzuela told me, by the fact that whatever the season, the temperature indoors was a blessed relief from the heat or chill outside. "All for half what a conventional building would have cost us," Valenzuela estimated.

"So is everyone here starting to build like this?" I asked.

His broad smile collapsed. "Banks won't give credit for this kind of building. They say it needs to be brick or reinforced concrete."

"Can't you convince them? Have any bankers come to see this?"

"The banks are all headquartered in Mexico City. It's a long way from here. That's where they make the decisions. Not locally. The only hope is to get rich families interested."

Which might work with a charity, but not for everyone else, as Bill and Athena Steen learned from the laborers who had worked on the showpiece straw-bale office they'd just completed. Much of the finish detail work was done by women who were hired to build and plaster bookshelves and benches from mud and straw, and to paint murals with colored clays mixed with wheat paste. When the building was finally done, a group of them approached the Steens with a request.

They were, they explained, from Xochitl, a squalid settlement on the fringe of Obregón. Several had come from states to the south seeking agricultural work, but it paid poorly, and many of their husbands had ended up sneaking into the United States. The women and their children lived in houses pieced together from scrap wood, metal, cardboard, and tar paper. Could the Steens show them how to construct homes out of straw bales? If they helped them build one, the women said, they would learn and do the rest themselves. They had already decided who would get the first one: a mother of four whose husband was in jail.

Again, the Steens were willing. But they soon found that even the modest price of baled straw, whose costs include baling wire and diesel to power tractors to collect it, proved beyond these people's means. Save the Children, whose own bales had been donated, offered to help secure more. But to provide adequate substitute building materials for the millions of poor families in Mexico, donations would only go so far.

Yet sooner or later, the Steens figured, Mexico would desperately need such materials. On a drive around the outskirts of the city, they showed me the current unsustainable version of Mexico's housing future: Thousands of federally funded housing units, built of concrete block and steel reinforcing bar, were rising in former wheat fields. Typically, they averaged five hundred square feet and contained a cramped living room, a kitchen, a bath, and a pair of tiny bedrooms. To either side of each unit, barely a meter apart, identical structures spread for miles.

"There's a trillion of them," said Athena, gaping. "All with zero insulation."

"In hot months, people will swelter in these things," said Bill. "There's no room to breathe."

Nevertheless, Mexico was building hundreds of thousands of such cubes a year, trying to meet its exploding housing demand. The units came with twenty-year federal mortgages garnished from workers' paychecks. Their price, around US$20,000, represented about a tenfold markup from actual construction costs, Bill Steen guessed.

By contrast, he estimated, the houses being built by the Xochitl women, who had no paychecks, cost at most five hundred dollars. Leaving the concrete onslaught encircling Ciudad Obregón, we followed an arroyo fed by irrigation runoff to a lake now nearly dry from chronic drought, where their families squatted. Amid a jumble of cardboard and tin shacks stood nine snug new houses that would not have looked out of place in fashionable Santa Fe, New Mexico. Built from straw bales that Save the Children had provided, reinforced with bamboo rods, they resembled classic flat-roofed pueblo-style adobes. Their facades were plastered with a pastel rainbow of local clays hardened with lime discarded from a local acetylene plant. Their interiors featured polished floors of earth plaster imbedded with chunks of discarded broken concrete that resembled ornamental flagstone. Built-in plastered shelves, benches, and even beds had been sculpted from mud and straw. Ceilings were lined with bamboo or cactus ribs, and decorative wall niches held candles, photographs, and mirrors.

Even more impressive, however, was what was going on outside. In the afternoon shade of a lofty mesquite, five women stood at vats made from fifty-five-gallon drums sliced lengthwise, up to their elbows in chocolaty muck. As they kneaded wet earth through their fingers, children added wheelbarrow-loads of free straw from surrounding fields. When the blend was right, teenage girls pressed it with cookie-cutter-style wooden forms into bricks.

119

Unlike typically dense adobe blocks, however, these were more straw than mud: about a sixty-forty ratio. The Xochitl builders had discovered a mixture that produced cost-free bricks that were far lighter than conventional adobes but replicated the additional insulating qualities of straw bales. Their high straw content also made them water resistant; yet they were strong enough to use for the two-story church they had nearly finished.

Straw-mud bricks had made further donations of straw bales unnecessary. "They can also be cut without crumbling," Xochitl resident Juanita López told me. She was watching her husband, Emiliano, wield a machete to shape bricks for arched windows to echo the vaulted roof on the house he was building for his mother. Emiliano said that he was home to stay. He took me to see their latest straw-mud architectural achievement: a round dome, inspired by the photograph of an ancient Egyptian granary Bill Steen had showed him.

"We're making it the way they did. To last."

THE FOLLOWING DAY, the Steens took me to an upperclass neighborhood to meet Beatriz Marina Bours de Pineda, president of the Yaqui Valley Social Welfare Committee, a Ciudad Obregón charity. She had visited the Save the Children office and Xochitl and decided that "this was exactly the kind of project we should be promoting to help meet the basic needs of our community." Her organization had been seeking grants from international funding agencies for extremely low-interest housing loans for poor people. Now they were leveraging funds to pay people to make straw-clay bricks to build their own houses.

"We pay them so that they can then afford their houses." Already, 360 straw-brick houses in three barrios were underway or already completed. "Nobody has defaulted. They love their naturally insulated houses. Even if it's only five pesos a month, they're motivated to pay." She was talking to the Inter-American Development Bank about financing 190 more. "That's more than five hundred total," she said, pouring us more tea. "Now we're getting into big numbers."

Joining us in her spacious living room was her husband, Guillermo Pineda, who introduced himself as a civil engineer with INFONAVIT, Mexico's federal housing authority—the agency that was building the thousands of cloned, low-income housing units surrounding the city.

"Do you two fight a lot?" I asked him and his wife. They laughed, holding hands on the satin couch. How did they feel about each other's efforts, I insisted. Did Guillermo believe there was any chance that earthen houses could replace concrete cubicles?

Not really, he replied. "These mud-straw houses are principally for people living in cardboard shacks. Right now, they build four per month. Meanwhile, as a country we have a deficit of 760,000 housing units we need to build annually, which we haven't fulfilled. Unfortunately, economics limit us to what we have. INFONAVIT has specifications for acceptable materials, and adobe is not one of them."

He listed what he called the "traditional materials we use in Mexico: bricks, concrete cinderblock, concrete slabs, concrete roofs, concrete domes with polystyrene." As he spoke, I envisioned all the eighteen-wheel trucks I'd seen on Mexican highways, burning diesel from Mexico's national petroleum company, PEMEX, to move all those heavy concrete blocks across the country. Cement is one of Mexico's biggest industries. So many Mexican jobs, I realized, were tied up in the production and transport of those "traditional materials" that Mexico's economy might simply collapse if everyone built their houses out of the mud beneath their feet.

I mentioned the roar of dump trucks, cement mixers, and jackhammers at the huge new INFONAVIT housing project the Steens and I had visited, compared with the construction site at Xochitl, where only hand tools were needed and the main sound was children's laughter.

"Yes," agreed Pineda, "there should be eco-friendly alternatives to jackhammers. But there's so much invested in them. People who profit don't want things to change."

122

"IT ALSO BOTHERS me," he admitted as we left, "how uniform it all is, and how small the housing units are. There's a loss of identity. You see people painting their houses, trying to individualize them."

Bill and Athena Steen, of Mexican and Native American descent, respectively, find it ironic that they were invited to Sonora to reconnect Mexicans with indigenous building techniques their own ancestors invented thousands of years earlier. They have noted that Xochitl residents who once again live in houses built of their own earth and labor, poor as they may be, have no desire to flee Mexico for the United States: their homes, as beautiful in their own right as indigenous ceramics that the Quezadas have resurrected at Mata Ortiz, are too deliciously comfortable to leave behind.

"For them to now go live in another culture surrounded by anonymous concrete walls," says Bill Steen, "would simply be too painful a step backwards."

Uncompromising

DEDICATION

Over the half-century of my lifetime,

the planet has changed beyond belief—

the once-vast assemblages of wildlife

and seemingly endless ancient forests have

been drastically reduced to mere vestiges of

what they were. We know with absolute certainty

that our children will inherit a world with

radically diminished biological diversity

and extensive global pollution of air, water,

and soil. If we do love our children, what excuse

can we possibly have for not pulling out all stops

to try to ensure that things don't get worse?

{ DAVID SUZUKI }

TOWARD A REAL
KYOTO PROTOCOL

——— *Ross Gelbspan* ———

IF WORLD LEADERS HAD A FRACTION OF DAVID SUZUKI'S
vision and commitment, they would long ago have
embraced a plan to reduce carbon emissions globally by
the 70 percent required by nature. (According to the Inter-
governmental Panel on Climate Change [IPCC], that is the
scale of reductions needed to allow the climate to stabilize.) And they would have done it in a way that would
create millions of jobs around the world, especially in
developing countries.

The need for humanity to reach this goal is glaringly
obvious: the deep oceans are warming, the tundra is
thawing, the glaciers are melting, infectious diseases are
migrating, and the timing of the seasons has changed.
And all of these changes have resulted from *one degree*
of warming. According to the IPCC, the Earth will warm
from three to ten degrees later in this century.

We need a properly funded global energy transition. As NASA scientist Jim Hansen wrote in the *Independent* in February 2006: "We have to stabilize emissions of carbon dioxide *within a decade,* or temperatures will warm by more than one degree—warmer than it has been for half a million years."

About seven years ago, I presented a series of ideas for an effective transition to a group of energy company executives, economists, and climate and energy policy specialists. Together we refined and polished the ideas and developed a plan that I believe—at the risk of exaggerating its potential—could address not only the effects of climate change but several other major problems facing us as well.

The most obvious effect of implementing this plan, given our newfound vulnerability to guerrilla attacks, is that a worldwide transition to renewable energy would dramatically reduce the significance of oil—and with it our exposure to the political volatility in the Middle East. In addition, a renewable energy economy would have far more independent sources of power,—home-based fuel cells, stand-alone solar systems, regional wind farms— which would make the nation's electricity grid a far less strategic target for terrorist attacks.

The continuing indifference to climate change by the United States—which generates a quarter of the world's carbon emissions—will likely provoke more guerrilla attacks from people whose homelands are going under from rising seas, whose crops are being destroyed by weather extremes, and whose borders are being overrun by environmental refugees. A properly funded global energy transition would represent the kind of proactive policy needed to begin to redress the economic inequity that threatens to split humanity irreparably between rich and poor. Just as runaway carbon concentrations threaten to destabilize the global climate, runaway economic inequity can only continue to destabilize our global political environment.

For its own security, the United States needs to replace its traditional posture toward developing countries—which has been by turns defensive and coercive—with a new set of policies that are expansive and inclusive and are geared toward alleviating poverty. It seems to be an article of faith among development economists that energy investments in poor countries create far more wealth and jobs than investments in any other sector. A U.S.-led transfer of clean-energy technologies to developing countries would do more than anything else in the long term to undermine support for anti-U.S. terrorism.

On the economic front, it seems clear the entire global economy is susceptible to periods of stagnation, even recession. Not long ago, some members of the Federal Reserve were even talking about deflation. A truly floundering economy seems relatively immune to tax cuts and interest-rate reductions. Any recipe for stable, long-term economic health must include a component of public works programs, and a program to rewire the globe with clean energy would be the most productive investment we could make in our future. Within a decade, it would begin to generate a major and continuing worldwide economic lift-off.

Finally, there is the climate crisis itself. Unintentionally, we have set in motion massive systems of the planet with huge amounts of inertia that have kept it relatively hospitable to civilization for the last 10,000 years. We have reversed the carbon cycle by more than 400,000 years. We have heated the deep oceans. We have loosed a wave of violent and chaotic weather. We have altered the timing of the seasons. We are living on a very precarious margin of stability.

Against that background, we—the group of industry experts and consultants and I—are offering the following set of strategies. We believe these strategies present a model of the scope and scale of action that is appropriate to the magnitude of the climate crisis. To date we have not seen other policy recommendations that adequately address either the scope or the urgency of the problem.

Largely because of inaction by the world's governments, it seems that the Kyoto goals (but *not* the Kyoto process) are fast becoming obsolete and that it will soon be time to go straight for the goal of 70 percent reductions globally. Our hope is to get our plan adopted and to get ideas of the scope that we are presenting into the conversation and to help move that conversation to an appropriate level.

The plan involves three interacting strategies, which include:

· a subsidy switch: in industrial countries the withdrawal of subsidies from fossil fuels and the establishment of equivalent subsidies for clean energy sources;

· an energy modernization fund: the creation of a large fund—perhaps through a small tax on global commerce—to transfer clean energy technologies to developing countries; and,

· a progressive fossil-fuel-efficient standard: the incorporation within the Kyoto framework of a progressively more stringent standard that rises by 5 percent per year.

SUBSIDY SWITCH

The United States currently spends more than 20 billion dollars a year to subsidize fossil fuels. In the industrial countries overall, those subsidies have been estimated at 200 billion dollars a year.

We propose that, in the industrial countries, those subsidies be withdrawn from fossil fuels, and equivalent subsidies be established to promote the development of clean energy sources. (Clearly, a small portion of the U.S. subsidies must be used to retrain or buy out the nation's fifty thousand or so coal miners.) But the lions' share of the subsidies would still be available for use by the major oil companies to retrain their workers and retool to become aggressive developers of fuel cells, wind farms, and solar systems. At the same time, we would see the emergence of an army of energy engineers and entrepreneurs—with successively more efficient generations of solar film, turbines, and tidal devices—in a burst of creativity that would rival the dot-com explosion of the 1990s.

But even if the countries of the North were to reduce emissions dramatically, those cuts would be overwhelmed by the coming pulse of carbon from India, China, Mexico, and Nigeria. Therefore the second element of the plan involves the creation of a fund of about 300 billion dollars a year for several years to jumpstart renewable-energy infrastructures in developing countries. Virtually all poor countries would love to go solar; virtually none can afford it. The most air-polluted cities in the world today are in China, Mexico, Thailand, Chile, and other developing and transitional countries.

ENERGY MODERNIZATION FUND

The size of the fund was calculated by energy policy specialists at the Tellus Institute, a blue-ribbon energy policy think tank. It could be financed by any number of mechanisms. One attractive source is a tax on international currency transactions, named after its developer, the late Nobel Prize-winning economist Dr. James Tobin. Although Tobin conceived his tax as a way of damping the volatility in capital markets, it would also generate enormous revenues. Today the commerce in currency swaps amounts to 1.5 trillion dollars per day. A tax of a quarter-penny on a dollar would net out to about 300 billion dollars a year for wind farms in India, fuel-cell factories in South Africa, solar assemblies in El Salvador, and vast, solar-powered hydrogen farms in the Middle East.

Since currency transactions are electronically tracked by the private banking system, the need for a large, new bureaucracy could be avoided by paying the banks a fee to administer the fund. That fee could, to a large extent, offset their loss of income from the contraction in currency trading that would result from the tax. And the involvement of the banks in administering the fund would go a long way toward minimizing corruption and ensuring that the money would go directly to clean energy projects.

The only new bureaucracy required would be an international auditing agency to ensure equal access for all energy vendors and to minimize corruption in recipient countries. Several commentators from developing countries have suggested that corruption could be further curtailed by requiring recipient governments to include representatives of indigenous minorities, universities, NGOs, and labor unions in their decisions about procuring new energy resources.

If a currency transaction tax proves unacceptable, a carbon tax in industrial countries or a tax on international airline travel could fulfill the same function. Economists

133

estimate that if carbon emissions were taxed at the rate of fifty dollars a ton, the revenue would approximate the 300 billion dollars from a tax on currency transactions.

Regardless of its revenue source, the fund—on the ground—would be allocated according to a United Nations formula to determine what percentage of each year's fund would go to each developing country. If India, for instance, were to receive five billion dollars in the first year, it would decide what mix of wind farms, village solar installations, fuel cell generators, and biogas facilities it wanted, and the Indian government would entertain bids for these facilities. As contractors reached specified benchmarks, they would be paid directly by the banks.

As self-replicating renewable infrastructures took root in developing countries, the fund could simply be phased out. Alternatively, progressively larger amounts of the fund could be diverted to other global environment and development needs.

PROGRESSIVE FOSSIL FUEL EFFICIENCY STANDARD

The third and unifying strategy of the plan—which makes it all work—calls on the parties to Kyoto to subordinate the uneven and inequitable system of international emissions trading to a simple and equitable progressively more stringent fossil fuel efficiency standard, which goes up by about 5 percent per year. This mechanism, if incorporated into the Kyoto Protocol, would harmonize and guide the global energy transition in a way that emissions trading cannot.

Even if all the shortcomings in monitoring, enforcement, and equity could be resolved, international carbon trading would most appropriately be used as a fine-tuning instrument—to help countries attain the final 10 to 15 percent of their obligations. It is not the workhorse vehicle required to propel a worldwide energy transition; we simply can't finesse nature with accounting tricks.

The fossil fuel efficiency standard would be simple to negotiate, easy to monitor, and ultimately fair. (National "cap-and-trade" regimes could be useful in helping countries meet the progressive standard.) Under this mechanism, every country would start at its current baseline to increase its fossil fuel energy efficiency by 5 percent every year until the global 70 percent reduction is attained. That means a country would produce the same amount of goods as the previous year with 5 percent less carbon fuel. Alternatively, it would produce 5 percent more goods with the same carbon fuel use as the previous year.

Since no economy grows at 5 percent for long, emissions reductions would outpace long-term economic growth. For the first few years of the efficiency standard, most countries would likely meet their goals by implementing low-cost or even profitable efficiencies—the "low-hanging fruit"—in their current energy systems. After a few years, however, as those efficiencies became more expensive to capture, countries would meet the progressively more stringent standard by drawing more and more energy from noncarbon sources—most of which are 100 percent efficient by a fossil fuel standard.

135

That development, in turn, would create the mass markets and economies of scale for renewables that would bring down their prices and make them competitive with coal and oil. This approach would be far simpler to negotiate than the current protocol, with its morass of details involving emissions trading, reviews of the adequacy of commitments, and differentiated targets. It would also be far easier to monitor. A nation's compliance would be measured simply by calculating the annual change in the ratio of its carbon fuel use to its gross domestic product. That ratio would have to change by 5 percent a year.

This approach has a precedent in the Montreal Protocol, under which companies phased out ozone-destroying chemicals. That protocol was successful because the same companies that made the destructive chemicals were able to produce their substitutes with no loss of competitive standing within the industry. An energy transition must be regulated in the same way. Several oil executives have said in private conversations that they can, in an orderly fashion, de-carbonize their energy supplies. But they need the governments of the world to regulate the process so that all companies can make the transition in lockstep without losing market share to competitors. A progressive fossil fuel efficiency standard would provide that type of regulation.

The plan, then, would be driven by these three engines: the subsidy switch would propel the metamorphosis of oil companies into energy companies; the progressive fossil fuel efficiency standard would harmonize the transformation of national energy structures and create a level field of predictable regulation for the major energy corporations; and the competition for the new 300-billion-dollars-a-year market in clean energy would power the whole process.

A plan of this magnitude—regardless of the details—would create millions of jobs, especially in developing countries. It would turn impoverished and dependent countries into trading partners. It would raise living standards abroad without compromising North American standards. It would undermine the economic desperation that gives rise to so much anti-U.S. sentiment. And in a very short time, it would jump the renewable-energy industry into a central, driving engine of growth of the global economy.

Stepping back for a moment to a wider-angle vantage point, this kind of initiative could also be the beginning of the end of an outdated and increasingly toxic nationalism, which we have long ago outgrown.

Finally, and at the risk of being overly visionary, I do believe that because energy is so central to our existence, a common global project to rewire the world with clean energy could be the first step on a path to peace—even in today's profoundly fractured world: peace among people and peace between people and nature.

The economy is becoming truly globalized. The globalization of communications now makes it possible for any person to communicate with anyone else around the

137

world. And since it does not respect national boundaries, the global climate makes us all one.

We hear many complaints about the costliness of addressing the climate crisis. But the real economic issue in rewiring the world with clean energy is not cost. The real economic issue is whether the world has a large enough labor force to accomplish this task in time to meet nature's deadline.

And therein lies the catch—nature's deadline. A growing number of the world's leading climate scientists agree that we are already too far along a catastrophic trajectory to avoid significant disruptions. So my enthusiasm for the healing potential—on many levels—of something like these solutions is tempered by an increasingly loud and persistent question: How are people of good will and social conscience supposed to respond in the face of a coming age of collapse?

There is no body of expertise—no authoritative answers—for this one. We are crossing a threshold into uncharted territory. And since there is no precedent to guide us, we are left with only our own hearts to consult, the intellectual integrity to look reality in the eye, whatever courage we can muster, and our uncompromising dedication to a human future that reflects the combined aspirations of every single reader of this essay.

WHY WE SHOULD
CARE ABOUT THE OCEAN

—— *Heike K. Lotze & Boris Worm* ——

SOMETIMES WE NEED TO REMIND OURSELVES WHERE we live. Our planet is the planet of life and the planet of the ocean. We know of no other planet that supports life as Earth does, and no other planet has an ocean like ours. The ocean covers 70 percent of our planet's surface and makes up more than 90 percent of the biosphere, much of it in the deep sea. It is the ocean where life itself emerged. It is the ocean where our planet unfolds most of its diversity, in a stunning variety of colors and shapes of all life-forms. It is the ocean where large parts of the planet's life-support system are housed, and that provides food for billions of people. It is the ocean that shaped our lives and myths. Long taken for granted and deemed inexhaustible, it is the ocean that needs our care today.

THE ORIGIN AND FUTURE OF LIFE

"And as life itself began in the sea, so each of us begins his individual life in a miniature ocean within his mother's womb, and in the stages of his embryonic development repeats the steps by which his race evolved, from gill-breathing inhabitants of a water world to creatures able to live on land." —Rachel Carson, *The Sea Around Us*

LIFE AS WE know it originated in the ocean and remained there for the first 3 billion years of evolution, until the first organisms made their way onto land 400 million years ago. As a result, we find a much greater variety of life-forms in the sea than on land. Of all major animal groupings (phyla), more than 90 percent are represented in the sea and almost 50 percent occur exclusively there. Today, however, we only know about 250,000 marine species, compared with 1.5 million terrestrial ones. In its wide and often hidden reaches, the ocean likely harbors a tremendous unknown diversity of life-forms, especially in the deep sea and within coral reefs. Each year hundreds of new species are brought to light, but thousands, maybe millions, more remain undiscovered.

Whether a minuscule plankton organism, a colorful jelly, a dragonlike fish from the abyss, or a giant whale— all species attest to the miracle of evolution. They live and move with the seasons of the sea. Some dwell in environments utterly unfamiliar to us, such as deep-sea hydrothermal vents. Others, such as the great whales, tunas, albatrosses, and sea turtles, travel across entire ocean basins as part of their seasonal routine. Each species, whether on land or in the sea, is a unique expression of life itself. It represents one line of evolution that was successful in surviving a tumultuous past, and it carries the potential to play an important part in the future of life on our planet. With every species we lose, we put an end to a distinct line of evolution and to a range of future options.

Through its evolution each species came to inhabit a distinct niche in the web of life. Hence every species has developed a unique way to adapt to the environmental problems of its time, whether those problems are predators, food shortages, or climatic extremes. Likewise each of these species will have its unique response to future environmental changes. At the same time, every species fulfills a specific ecological role in sustaining the web of life today, whether as prey or predator, habitat provider or waste recycler. Tightly connected in a web of weak and strong links, all these species together stabilize the composition and functioning of the ocean ecosystem. Thereby they also secure the flow of natural goods and services that humans depend on, such as fisheries, coastal protection, and climate regulation. Disrupting the interconnected variety of marine life poses threats to the ocean, to humanity, and to the future of life.

OUR SECOND BREATH

The ocean and its inhabitants support, regulate, and stabilize the planet's life-support system. About half of the global primary production occurs in the ocean, most of it produced by single-celled algae called phytoplankton, the rest by a colorful melange of seaweeds, seagrasses, kelps, and mangroves. As by-products of photosynthesis, these organisms produce half of the oxygen on this planet. We may think of every second breath we take as coming from the ocean.

There are thousands of known species of algae in the ocean. Apart from producing oxygen, these plants consume carbon and nutrients to create organic material, the food base on which all life in the ocean depends. If not eaten, the algae sink toward the seafloor, transporting food, carbon, and nutrients into the deep sea sink. Importantly, that material stays deep down for thousands of years and does not contribute to the greenhouse effect. Thus these tiny algae feed the ocean's life and stabilize the climate—a big task. Experiments show that a diverse assemblage of plants increases the productivity of the plants themselves and the animals that eat them, and it increases the efficiency of resource use. Moreover, the larger seaweeds, seagrasses, kelps, and mangroves provide a variety of habitats for the spawning and breeding, nursing and foraging, and resting and sheltering of animals. We may think of them as the gardens and forests of the sea.

SEAFOOD FOR THOUGHT

Since ancient times, people have lived from the sea. They have valued a large variety of seafood, ranging from fish and shellfish to waterfowl, whales, and seals. They have also relied on furs and skins for clothing, feathers and shells for ornaments, bones for tools, and oil for keeping a fire and providing light. Many of these uses have been replaced with other, nonliving resources. But most people still value a wide variety of wild seafood, and many rely on fish for their main source of protein.

According to a recent report from the Food and Agriculture Organization of the United Nations (FAO), about 15 to 16 percent of world animal protein consumption comes from fish protein. On average, in 2004, every person on the planet consumed about 16.6 kilograms of fish, the highest amount on record. Seafood can be a healthful diet choice, and the omega-3 acids that are particularly concentrated in fish have recently made headlines as brain food. But persistent pollutants such as mercury and PCBs, which accumulate in the food chain, can make some large predators such as tuna, sharks, and swordfish dangerous for human consumption, especially for children and pregnant women. Fish and shellfish are sometimes contaminated from water pollution or poisoned by toxic algae. Aquaculture-grown fish also come with a toll. As in intense animal farming, pesticides and antibiotics are often used and can find their way into the surrounding environment and the human food chain.

The availability of seafood and the circumstances of its capture or farming provide food for thought. Again according to the FAO report, fisheries and aquaculture supplied the world with a total of 106 million tonnes of food fish in 2004. Of this, aquaculture produced 43 percent, and that number is increasing. Global fisheries landings in turn have been declining since the late 1980s, and the percentage of overfished and collapsed fish stocks has increased from 10 percent in the 1970s to 25 percent in the 1990s.

Dwindling marine resources are not entirely a recent phenomenon but have a long history. For example, prehistoric people were already depleting fur seals around New Zealand and oysters, sturgeon, geese, and sea otters in San Francisco Bay. Ancient Romans heavily fished Mediterranean coastal waters 2,500 years ago, and medieval people did the same around the North and Baltic seas 1,000 years ago. European colonizers then exported their fisheries practices to the New World as they searched for more fish, furs, feathers, and fuel. Hence coastal seas have been transformed for many centuries, but only over the last fifty years have these effects spread across the open ocean and into the deep sea. Our grip on the ocean has become global.

Throughout history people responded to dwindling resources with similar management strategies, most of which are still applied today. To supplement locally depleted stocks, fisheries moved somewhere else: farther offshore and deeper into the lightless reaches of the continental slopes and the deep sea. Another "solution" was to fish down the food chain; this practice means substituting large fish such as tuna and cod with smaller and less valued fish and invertebrate species. In Nova Scotia, where fishermen once landed giant bluefin tuna, cod, and halibut, there is now much excitement about sea cucumbers, slime eels, and shrimp. To catch the dwindling species, fishing techniques have often become more powerful and less selective, with the inherent problems of unintended by-catch and the disturbance of sensitive seafloor habitats. Finally, declining wild fish are being replaced by increasing aquaculture production, yet much of this production still depends on wild-caught ground-up fish for feed.

Fish and fisheries are not divorced from the ocean they inhabit. They are supported by the entire variety of marine life, which provides sufficient food, habitat, and good water quality as well as building a network of interconnected species . Often the species that we most value as food can play important roles in themselves, regulating marine food chains from the top, much as wolves and lions do on land. We recently found that ocean regions that harbor a greater richness of fish species are more robust and resilient to fishing, and tend to be more productive in the long term, than ocean regions with fewer fish species. High species diversity acts as a buffer and stabilizer, resulting in a reduced risk of fisheries collapse and quicker recovery after a collapse. This situation is similar to an investment portfolio, where diversity insures a reduced risk of financial loss. In the ocean more species make the entire system more productive, stable, and resilient. To keep the whole functioning, it is wise not to lose any of the parts.

THE MYTHICAL SEA

Throughout history, human cultures and religions around the world have been influenced, inspired, and shaped by the ocean and its inhabitants. Whales, dolphins, and sharks have prominent places in many myths, stories, dances, and artworks of indigenous people. For example, the Hula of Hawaii refer to the shark god Kamohoali'i, the Kuna Yala of Panama tell stories of guardian shark spirits who protect fishermen, and the Yolngu people of Northern Australia believe that shark ancestors helped create the world and consider sharks and rays sacred. Along the coasts of the seven seas, fishermen and fishing communities identify with the sea and its inhabitants. In Newfoundland, for example, Atlantic cod and its fishery have shaped communities for many centuries. The recent collapse of the cod fishery creates a void that goes beyond financial hardship. For most of us, the living ocean enhances enjoyment, recreation, artistic and spiritual fulfillment, and intellectual development. Many of these cultural benefits have been impoverished by the depletion of marine life and degradation of coastal seas. The decline of ocean wildlife leaves a sense of loss.

TURNING THE TIDE

146

How do we care for something as vast as the ocean? How can we break our pathological habit of serial depletion, destruction, and pollution? How can we turn toward recovery, restoration, and sustainable use of the ocean's resources? There are several ways to go. We can start by learning from existing success stories. We can begin making informed choices and decisions in our everyday lives. And we can develop a sense of stewardship and governance for our oceans.

Success stories of turning depletion and degradation into recovery exist. Strict management to reduce nutrient pollution enabled the recovery of seagrass beds in Tampa Bay, Florida, and the comeback of fish species in some Great Britain estuaries. Protection of breeding and migratory habitats together with reduced hunting pressure helped numerous waterfowl, seabirds, and shorebirds to recover from low levels over the past decades. The banning of DDT helped raptors such as bald eagles and peregrine falcons to regain population strength. Hunting restrictions and habitat protection supported the recovery of sea otters and elephant seals in California and harbor and gray seals in the North Sea. In some countries such as the United States, laws have been crafted that make it illegal to overfish and that mandate rebuilding of depleted fish stocks. Maybe for the first time in history, the conservation, not the exploitation, of fisheries takes center stage. An increasing number of marine reserves or areas closed to fishing aid the recovery of depleted fish and invertebrate stocks, such as haddock and scallops on Georges Bank in New England. Combined with stricter regulation of fishing effort and quotas, area closures could help restore depleted fisheries around the globe. Furthermore, marine parks could serve as refuges for threatened species and insurance in the face of environmental change.

Each of us can help to sustain the ocean's richness by making informed decisions in our day-to-day lives. Many organizations have published wallet-sized cards that provide information about the status of seafood species, the circumstances of their capture, and existing health concerns in Canada (www.seachoice.org), the United States (www.montereybayaquarium.org), and Europe and Asia (www.panda.org). In addition, the Marine Stewardship Council certifies sustainable fisheries and seafood with the MSC label (www.msc.org). These sustainable seafood products are available for the wholesale market, restaurants, and citizens. Our informed choice is making an impact.

Developing a sense of stewardship for the ocean is necessary and possible. Plans to develop sustainable management strategies exist, and principles for sustainable governance have been outlined, at least on paper. But so far only 1 percent of the ocean is protected from human activities, compared with 12 percent on land. Despite our recent progress, many coastal seas continue to be polluted, many habitats are still being destroyed, and many fish stocks are still being depleted every day. We have to learn quickly. Our oceans need better governance and care. This is our chance, our challenge, and our responsibility.

SAVE THE ENVIRONMENT—
TAKE BACK THE MEDIA

Doug Moss

IN APRIL 2006 TV COMEDY SHOW HOST STEPHEN Colbert closed the annual White House Correspondents' Dinner with a sarcastic speech that ridiculed both the Bush administration and the U.S. press corps as they were finishing their dessert. A video of his remarks spread rapidly across the Internet and became a subject of much debate on TV. Most of the controversy dealt with the acerbic nature of his remarks, delivered just two place settings away from President and Laura Bush.

But as caustic as Colbert's remarks were, they could have been much more critical of the press community itself, which was his captive audience for the evening. He got in a few good cracks, such as: "Over the last five years you people were so good—over tax cuts, WMD intelligence, the effect of global warming. We Americans didn't want to know, and you had the courtesy not to try to find out." But for the most part, Colbert avoided any real analysis of how the media in America have degenerated into a mean-spirited and cynical circus of entertainment, titillation, spin, and lies (including major lies of omission), masquerading as journalism.

Writing in the *Providence Journal* last year, Quinnipiac University adjunct professor of journalism John Motavalli observed that most of the liberal viewpoints reaching the mainstream these days are doing so through the venue of comedy, like Colbert's own show, *The Colbert Report*. Although I disagree with his conclusions, which suggest that liberals (including environmentalists) stand for nothing today and are just "against everything," his initial observation was spot on. Colbert, *Real Time with Bill Maher*, *The Daily Show with Jon Stewart*, Al Franken, Janeane Garofalo, Arianna Huffington—where else are liberal views, including pro-environmental ones, articulated without being shouted down by the likes of Bill O'Reilly and Sean Hannity?

The right's appalling behavior deserves the stand-up spanking it gets, but this trend Motavalli spoke of does mean that progressive viewpoints, including those that seek to weigh in and enlighten the public about crucial environmental issues, have been largely relegated to the peanut gallery, a state of affairs that may actually be counterproductive. Why, for example, do O'Reilly, Chris Matthews, and other conservative pundits agree to appear on *The Daily Show* and *The Colbert Report*, venues you would think they'd shun as readily as George Bush avoids theaters showing *An Inconvenient Truth?* It is because the comedic element allows them to dismiss all charges as just lighthearted fun, not serious. The hosts treat them with kid gloves, and they go off almost completely unscathed, even looking good, when they should have been raked over the coals for the profound disservice they are doing to humanity.

This is a sorry state of affairs, and if the urgent environmental issues many of us work so hard to address are to get a fair hearing, we are going to need serious media reform. We shouldn't be fooled into thinking that anything has changed just because there is a temporary spike in interest in global warming. Besides, countless other ills persist as a result of longstanding media underreporting.

And we should also not believe for a second that changes will happen anytime soon without the full-fledged participation of the philanthropic (grant-making) community.

I liken the need for media reform with the need for election reform. In seeking election reform, we want good, decent people in power, people who truly serve global interests and not just special interests. And we go on faith that if the system were to be made fair, that would naturally occur. Similarly, in media reform we simply need a much larger bloc of progressive media that will balance the right's juggernaut. If they had the chance, equal time, "liberal" positions would be well expressed instead of shouted down, and, I believe, the public would find them reasonable—without the need for punch lines.

But trying to reform media by enacting legislation to halt consolidation of media ownership, revamp Federal Communications Commission (FCC) rulemaking, force media to be accountable to the public interest and not corporate interests, and provide equal and free time to political candidates could take a lifetime. These goals should still be pursued, for sure, but we should not delay in getting the ball rolling by bolstering those progressive media "points of light" already in place that face daily struggles to survive and compete in the marketplace of ideas. After all, what good is "media reform" theory without practice?

It's important to understand that conservative media don't need philanthropy's help, but liberal media do. The right's views generally meld well with the advertisers that will support it, just as it is a cakewalk for the sexy, make-no-waves editorial offerings of the fashion/sports/celebrity media to obtain mass readership. In contrast, because liberal views are often critical of accepted doctrine or downright depressing (but sorely in need of discussion nonetheless), they cannot survive in the advertising—or "cool"-driven—models.

Sheldon Rampton and John Stauber, in their 2004 book, *Banana Republicans,* argue that modern mass media have evolved into a "fourth branch of government," an astute observation, I think, considering the direction mass media have taken in recent years: see-no-evil "embedded reporters" in Iraq, softball questions dominating press conferences, Fox News as the White House's preferred network (and job candidate pool), and major radio networks like Clear Channel censoring musicians (like the Dixie Chicks) because of their political views. And we've recently learned that the Bush administration has been both paying columnists to promote official viewpoints and producing their own "news" segments for TV stations to run, without divulging the true origin. When the Soviet empire did this, we called it propaganda.

Look, too, what the "Swift Boat" people got away with during the last presidential election, with media as accomplices. Their lying ads appeared everywhere, while the major media outlets that ran them denied airtime to many a "Move On" ad that supported John Kerry. Moreover, the media then created a "news story" about the ad controversy, showing them over and over and over again in the process, likely giving them as much as ten or perhaps one hundred times the exposure they paid for.

A similar chain of events occurred more recently in relation to Democratic presidential candidate Barack Obama's alleged schooling at a Muslim *madrassa* school. A right-wing organization planted the story, and then Fox News, the Fox-owned *New York Post*, and Moonie-owned *Insight* magazine ran with it. Alhough CNN and other media quickly debunked the charge, such accusations tend to stick, which was the goal of those leaking the rumor.

Aside from the sheer magnitude of conservative programming in relation to liberal programming, progressive and pro-environmental media outlets must also compete with that great sea of media frivolity out there. Fashion, sports, and celebrity magazines ad nauseam, and their broadcast and online counterparts, have done such a good job of hypnotizing Americans that as ratings will show, they readily *choose* to know more about Tom Cruise's new baby than the threat of melting glaciers. Is it any wonder that the average American male is barely able to conduct more than a thirty-second conversation about anything but sports?

Many of us in environmental advocacy work followed the "Death of Environmentalism" controversy in late 2004 and early 2005, after a paper with that title was published. The authors said the movement's problems were largely a result of its leadership's inability to publicly articulate a clear vision. I think our movement actually does a pretty good job of laying out the problems and the needed solutions. But as long as the mainstream media, in cahoots with a conservative administration and other right-wing special interests, remain hell bent on discrediting or censoring any "liberal" or pro-environmental view, no variation on the spin is going to make a difference.

Nevertheless, there clearly endures a prejudice among environmental advocacy groups and the private liberal foundations that fund them that causes them to assign media a very low priority, largely because the impact of such work isn't immediately measurable. But these groups need to stand back and take a longer view. Media are among the strongest man-made forces known to humanity. And right now they are almost completely controlled by the conservative right. Although "never" is a strong word, I believe it is fair to say that those of us working hard for social, environmental, and economic change are never going to win our battles if we don't first (or concurrently) change that.

George Lakoff, the professor of linguistics at the University of California–Berkeley, whose work in large part inspired the "Death of Environmentalism" debate, has made some very astute observations about liberal philanthropy in relation to the right. He is particularly on the money in his analysis of the right's shrewd capacity/infrastructure-building support for media, contrasted with liberals' large avoidance of such efforts and preference for direct services.

Writing in his book *Don't Think of an Elephant: Know Your Values and Frame the Debate,* Lakoff says that liberal organizations have been "privatized by the right," relegated to doing the work that government should be doing, while, "in the right's hierarchy of moral values, the top value is preserving and defending the moral system itself."

I might add that it is no coincidence that conservatives are forever cutting social and environmental programs, pushing the burden instead onto the private sector, which largely includes private foundations. And I am also aware that the very origin of nonprofit 501(c)(3) status was to empower the private sector, by relieving it and its support base of certain tax obligations, to pick up the ball where the government was dropping it. But that is no more relevant today than the "right to keep and bear arms" that was extended over two hundred years ago when foreign aggression went door-to-door on foot. Conservative, anti-environmental nonprofits today bask in funding for their *advocacy* through media.

The Pacific Research Institute (PRI) is a case in point. Each year PRI publishes the "Index of Leading Environmental Indicators," which, hiding behind an objective title, argues that ecosystems are in much better condition than the "gloom and doom" environmentalists claim. (And to the extent that anything has improved, they give no acknowledgment to the role the "doom and gloom" sector played in forcing those improvements.) Editors around the nation publish and cite PRI's work as authoritative, when in fact it is highly one-note pitched in favor of free-market approaches. And they reach, directly or indirectly, a sizable portion of the population with their messages and are just one of numerous such organizations.

From PRI's own website:

In 2003, PRI reached a circulation of more than 100 million readers, with its commentary published in more than one thousand newspapers, magazines, and online outlets. PRI was featured by more than half of the nation's top one hundred print media, and was covered in all fifty states. PRI reached an audience of more than 23 million through radio and television nationwide . . . PRI policy staff has appeared on

NBC's "The Today Show," CNBC, CNN, MSNBC, and the Fox News Channel. PRI's work has been cited and published in the *Wall Street Journal, New York Times, Newsweek, Time, USA Today, The Economist, The Atlantic Monthly, Investor's Business Daily, Washington Times, Chicago Tribune, Los Angeles Times,* and many other leading publications throughout the world.

How many environmental advocacy groups can say the same of their work?

PRI's funders include the Lynde and Harry Bradley Foundation, the Walton Family Foundation, the Sarah Scaife Foundation, the ExxonMobil Foundation, the William H. Donner Foundation, and the John M. Olin Foundation, all known for their support for conservative causes and their very deep pockets. These foundations understand the need for organizations to speak their gospel free of funding worries.

Meanwhile, liberal organizations are left with little choice but to follow the money, pursuing grants "cherry-picked" in relation to foundations' stated narrow interests. Measurable results? Sometimes. Relevant to the long-term struggle? Not very often.

We need to fundamentally re-examine—in both environmental advocacy and funding circles—the notion that media efforts are just "talking" while other advocates are "doing." Case in point. I doubt that many people would dispute the notion that the recent upsurge in public interest in all things green is the end result of thousands of showings of the film *An Incovenient Truth*, a media project if there ever was one.

Will Rogers famously said, "I only know what I read in the newspapers." Social change is a process, not something that happens on Wednesday because we did something on Tuesday—and we need a continual marketplace presence to compete with all the wrong messages that are being repeated a thousand times a day.

The progressive philanthropic community needs to get behind efforts to reform media over the longer term while taking steps to bolster the health of the liberal media along the way. A Chinese proverb goes, "Give me a fish and I eat for a day. Teach me to fish and I eat for a lifetime." As this applies to the state of media affairs, we really need to do both—and to start right now—in order to level the playing field.

I'd go so far as to say that creating and building strong progressive media could well be the most important agenda item environmental and other social change activists have. Above all, it's time the funding community got the message.

FOOLS' PARADISE

Ronald Wright

THE GREATEST WONDER OF THE ANCIENT WORLD is how recent it really is. No city or monument is much more than five thousand years old. Only about seventy lifetimes, of seventy years, have been lived end to end since civilization began; its entire run occupies a mere 0.2 percent of the two and a half million years since our first ancestor sharpened a stone.

The progress of "man the hunter" during the Old Stone Age, or Paleolithic—his perfection of weapons and techniques—led directly to the end of hunting as a way of life. The big game was all but exterminated, except in a few places where conditions favored the prey. Next came the discovery of farming—likely by women—during the New Stone Age, or Neolithic, in several parts of the world. And from that grew the experiment of worldwide civilization, which began as many independent enterprises but over the last few centuries has coalesced, mainly by hostile takeover, into one big system that covers and consumes the Earth.

Not all past civilizations fell because of plague or conquest; many collapsed internally, victims of their own success after wearing out their welcome from the natural world. The wrecks of these failed experiments lie in deserts and jungles like fallen airliners whose flight recorders can tell us what went wrong. They are no longer of merely antiquarian interest. Civilization is now expanding at such a pace, and on such a scale, that we must understand its inherent patterns and dangers.

Archaeology is perhaps the best tool we have for looking ahead. Unlike written history, which is often highly edited, archaeology uncovers the deeds we have forgotten or have chosen to forget. It also offers a much longer reading of the direction and momentum of the human course through time. A realistic understanding of the past is quite a new thing, a late fruit of the Enlightenment, although people of many times have felt the tug of what the Elizabethan antiquarian William Camden called the "back-looking curiousity." Antiquity, he wrote, "hath a certaine resemblance with eternity. [It] is a sweet food of the mind." Not everyone's mind was so open in his day. An early Spanish viceroy of Peru who had just seen the Inca capital high in the Andes, with its walls of megaliths fitted like gems, wrote back to his king: "I have examined the fortress that [the Incas] built...which shows clearly

160

the work of the Devil . . . for it does not seem possible that
the strength and skill of men could have made it." Even
today, some opt for the comforts of mystification, preferring to believe that the wonders of the ancient world
were built by Atlanteans, gods, or space travelers instead
of by thousands toiling in the sun. Such thinking robs
our forerunners of their due and us of their experience.
Because then one can believe whatever one likes about
the past—without having to confront the bones, pot-
sherds, and inscriptions which tell us that people all over
the world, time and again, have made similar advances
and mistakes.

About two centuries after the Spanish invasion of
Peru, a Dutch fleet in the South Seas far to the west of
Chile and below the Tropic of Capricorn came upon a
sight hardly less awesome, and even more inexplicable,
than the megalithic buildings of the Andes. On Easter
Day 1722, the Dutchmen sighted an unknown island
so treeless and eroded they mistook its barren hills for
dunes. They were amazed, as they drew near, to see hundreds of standing stone images as tall as an Amsterdam
house. "We could not comprehend how it was possible
that these people, who are devoid of heavy thick timber
[or] strong ropes, nevertheless had been able to erect such
images, which were fully thirty feet high." Captain Cook
later confirmed the island's desolation, finding: "no wood
for fuel; nor any fresh water worth taking on board." He
described the islanders' tiny canoes, made from scraps
of driftwood stitched together like shoe leather, as the

worst in the Pacific. Nature, he concluded, had "been exceedingly sparing of her favours to this spot." The great mystery of Easter Island that struck all early visitors was not just that these colossal statues stood in such a tiny and remote corner of the world but that the stones seemed to have been put there without tackle, as if set down from the sky. The Spaniard who attributed the marvels of Inca architecture to the Devil was merely unable to recognize another culture's achievements. But even scientific observers could not, at first, account for the megaliths of Easter Island. The figures stood there mockingly, defying common sense.

We now know the answer to the riddle, and it is a chilling one. *Pace* Captain Cook, nature had not been unusually stingy with her favors. Pollen studies of the island's crater lakes have shown that it was once well watered and green, with rich volcanic soil supporting thick woods of the Chilean wine palm, a fine timber that can grow tall as an oak. No natural disaster had changed that: no eruption, drought, or disease. The catastrophe on Easter Island was man.

Rapa Nui, as Polynesians call the place, was settled during the fifth century AD by migrants from the Marquesas or the Gambiers, arriving in big catamarans stocked with their usual range of crops and animals: dogs, chickens, edible rats, sugarcane, bananas, sweet potatoes, and mulberry for making bark cloth. (Thor Heyerdahl's theory that the island was peopled from South America has not been supported by recent work, though sporadic contact between Peru and Oceania probably did take place.) Easter Island proved too cold for breadfruit and coconut palms but was rich in seafood: fish, seals, porpoises, turtles, and nesting seabirds. Within five or six centuries, the settlers multiplied to about ten thousand people—a lot for sixty-four square miles. They built villages with good houses on stone footings and cleared all the best land for fields. Socially they split into clans and ranks—nobles, priests, commoners—and there may have been a paramount chief or "king."

Like Polynesians on some other islands, each clan began to honor its ancestry with impressive stone images. These were hewn from the yielding volcanic tuff of a crater and set up on platforms by the shore. As time went on, the statue cult became increasingly rivalrous and extravagant, reaching its apogee during Europe's high Middle Ages, while the Plantagenet kings ruled England. Each generation of images grew bigger than the last, demanding more timber, rope, and manpower for hauling to the *ahu*, or altars. Trees were cut faster than they could grow, a problem worsened by the settlers' rats, who ate the seeds and saplings. By AD 1400, no more tree pollen is found in the annual strata of the crater lakes: the woods had been utterly destroyed by both the largest and the smallest mammal on the island.

We might think that in such a limited place where, from the height of Terevaka, islanders could survey their

163

whole world at a glance, steps would have been taken to halt the cutting, to protect the saplings, to replant. We might think that as trees became scarce, the erection of statues would have been curtailed and timber reserved for essential purposes such as boat building and roofing. But that is not what happened. The people who felled the last tree could *see* it was the last, could know with complete certainty that there would never be another. And they felled it anyway.

All shade vanished from the land except the hard-edged shadows cast by the petrified ancestors, whom the people loved all the more because they made them feel less alone. For a generation or so, there was enough old lumber to haul the great stones and still keep a few canoes seaworthy for deep water. But the day came when the last good boat was gone. The people then knew there would be little seafood and—worse—no way of escape. The word for wood, *rakau*, became the dearest in their language. Wars broke out over ancient planks and worm-eaten bits of jetsam. The people ate all their dogs and nearly all the nesting birds; and the unbearable stillness of the place deepened with animal silences. There was nothing left now but the *moai*, the stone giants who had devoured the land. And still these promised the return of plenty if only the people would keep faith and honor them with increase.

But how will we take you to the altars? asked the carvers, and the *moai* answered that when the time came they would walk there on their own. So the sound of hammering still rang from the quarries, and the crater walls came alive with hundreds of new giants, growing even bigger now they had no need of human transport. The tallest ever set on an altar is over thirty feet high and weighs eighty tons; the tallest ever *carved* is sixty-five feet long and more than *two hundred* tons, comparable to the greatest stones worked by the Incas or Egyptians. Except, of course, that it never moved an inch.

By the end there were more than a thousand *moai*, one for every ten islanders in their heyday. But the good days were gone—gone with the good earth, which had been carried away on the endless wind and washed by flash floods into the sea. The people had been seduced by a kind of progress that becomes a mania, an "ideological pathology," as some anthropologists call it. When Europeans arrived in the eighteenth century, the worst was over; they found only one or two living souls per statue, a sorry remnant, "small, lean, timid and miserable," in Cook's words. Now without roof beams, many people were dwelling in caves; their only buildings were stone henhouses, where they guarded this last nonhuman protein from each other day and night. The Europeans heard tales of how the warrior class had taken power, how the island had convulsed with burning villages, gory battles, and cannibal feasts. The one innovation of this end period was to turn the use of obsidian (a razor-keen volcanic glass) from toolmaking to weapons. Daggers and spearheads became the commonest artifacts on the island, hoarded in pits like the grenades and assault rifles kept by modern-day survivalists.

Even that was not quite the nadir. Between the Dutch visit of 1722 and Cook's fifty years later, the people again made war on each other and, for the first time, on the ancestors as well. Cook found *moai* toppled from their platforms, cracked and beheaded, the ruins littered with human bone. There is no reliable account of how or why this happened. Perhaps it started as the ultimate atrocity between enemy clans, like European nations bombing cathedrals in World War II. Perhaps it began with the shattering of the island's solitude by strangers in floating castles of unimaginable wealth and menace. These possessors of wood were also bringers of death and disease. Scuffles with sailors often ended with natives gunned down on the beach. We do not know exactly what promises had been made by the demanding *moai* to the people, but it seems likely that the arrival of an outside world might have exposed certain illusions of the statue cult, replacing compulsive belief with equally compulsive disenchantment.

Whatever its animus, the destruction on Rapa Nui raged for at least seventy years. Each foreign ship saw fewer upright statues, until not one giant was left standing on its altar. (Those standing today have been restored.) The work of demolition must have been extremely arduous for the few descendants of the builders. Its thoroughness

166

and deliberation speak of something deeper than clan warfare: of a people angry at their reckless fathers, of a revolt against the dead.

The lesson that Rapa Nui holds for our world has not gone unremarked. In the epilogue to their 1992 book, *Easter Island, Earth Island,* the archaeologists Paul Bahn and John Flenley are explicit. The islanders, they write

> carried out for us the experiment of permitting unre-
> stricted population growth, profligate use of resources,
> destruction of the environment and boundless confi-
> dence in their religion to take care of the future. The
> result was an ecological disaster leading to a popula-
> tion crash . . . Do we have to repeat the experiment on
> [a] grand scale? . . . Is the human personality always
> the same as that of the person who felled the last tree?

MAKING A DIFFERENCE

Jim Peacock & Shelly Peers

A CRISIS IN SCIENCE EDUCATION

In recent years secondary school students in Australia have shown a reduced interest in science. In the last two years of secondary school, when students are free to elect their subjects, fewer students choose to sign up for science and advanced mathematics courses. According to a 2001 report, between 1980 and 1998 the reduction in enrolments in biology, chemistry, and physics in year 12 (the final year of classes) was 25 percent, 13 percent, and 11 percent, respectively. As a result, enrolments for university science courses have also dropped. Australia is now seeing a shortage of people with appropriate skills to enter science-related careers, not only in research and teaching, but also in the many other exciting careers that stem from science and mathematics training.

When we looked for the origins of this problem, it was obvious that when children entered primary school they were excited about learning about the world around them. However, many of them appeared to lose interest in science by the time they entered secondary school, where science is mandatory for the first three or four years. When we examined primary school education in detail, it became clear that little time was spent teaching science. In some primary schools, science was not taught at all. On average only 41 minutes per week were spent teaching science, whereas 551 minutes were spent teaching English and literacy. Resources for teaching science were also limited. Unbelievably, anecdotal evidence indicates that the average science budget was fifty cents per student per year.

A WAY FORWARD

Various surveys brought the appalling trends into sharp focus. There was evidence that many primary school teachers avoided teaching science. The Australian Academy of Science embarked on designing a new way of teaching science in primary schools to provide teachers with appropriate resources and training, in the hopes of increasing their confidence and competence in teaching science to their eager pupils. Working closely with the Department of Education, Science and Training, the Academy put forward a proposal based on the premise that schools and teachers could be helped to teach science in an exciting way at the primary school level.

The Academy had already produced first-class materials for a structured program called Primary Investigations, first published in 1994. In 2002 the Academy and the Australian Department of Education, Science and Training commissioned a review of the program. According to the review, Primary Investigations had made a significant contribution to primary science education in Australia and that, with modification, it was likely to continue to provide a good foundation for promoting the teaching and learning of science in many Australian primary schools. The review recommended that the program retain many of its successful features, such as co-operative learning and the 5-Es approach, in which activities are presented in a sequence that passes through five phases: Engage, Explore, Explain, Elaborate, and Evaluate. Since students understand new information based on what they already know, activities should engage students and explore their own ideas before the teacher presents scientist's explanations. In the Elaborate phase, students apply their new science ideas in a scientific investigation before the outcomes of their learning are evaluated in the final phase.

AS A RESULT of the review, it also became clear that a less structured program that increased the interactions between teachers and students and included hands-on activities might be more effective. Further, efforts had to be made to improve the professional learning of the teachers, and all the state and territory departments of education and the science teacher associations had to be included in developing and implementing an updated program. The challenge was to persuade all of the education authorities in Australia to introduce science into their mainstream primary school courses. Additionally, if we wanted financial support from the Australian government to help the Academy develop the program, most or all of the different state authorities had to agree to making a request for support.

LINKING SCIENCE WITH LITERACY

We decided that we had to work within the system. We didn't think we could bring science into the school teaching programs if we had to make big changes in the way teaching operated in primary schools in the different states and territories. Because all primary schools, almost eight thousand in Australia, were required to teach a literacy block every day, we decided to provide to the teachers science units linked to the literacy program. This strategy would engage students and teachers in science and also have a positive impact on the literacy program. The education authorities and the science and literacy specialists all agreed with the idea—an almost unprecedented situation in Australia.

171

TRIAL PHASE

The next step was to form a reference group with representation from both science and literacy experts in all of the states and territories to produce science units that were appropriate to the literacy standards in the different years of primary schooling and that covered all the strands in the science curricula. One or two units were designed for each of the levels in primary school and were trialed in selected schools across Australia. A professional learning approach was also developed for teachers. We called this innovative program Primary Connections.

An independent review of the trial was very positive. A key finding was that teachers' confidence and professional capabilities were greatly increased. And most exciting, the students were highly engaged in the program and demonstrated increased levels of understanding of science concepts. This boost in understanding was unprecedented in Australian schools. All the authorities took a very positive view of the findings, and we began working with each of them to plan how to adopt the program.

AUSTRALIA-WIDE ACCEPTANCE

We were supported in this developmental phase by further funding from the Australian government. As the states and territories became more and more involved, their investment in the whole scheme became considerable. The interest in the program continues to expand, and requests for teacher training and the number of schools adopting the program are increasing rapidly in virtually all of the states and territories. Sales of the units for teachers are also increasing. These materials are extraordinarily exciting and cover the whole range of scientific disciplines that relate to the everyday experiences of the children.

Primary Connections has won the Australian Award for Excellence in Educational Publishing in the Teaching and Learning category for its quality and appropriateness for the purpose. Probably one of the most telling measures of success is just to be in the classroom where one of the units is being taught. The students are obviously excited and fully engaged in their investigations. It is marvelous to see their enthusiasm continue through each unit as they record their experiences—one of the main ways that their study of science interfaces with literacy.

PRIMARY CONNECTIONS UNITS

The units we developed are based on a matrix that is a synthesis of the curriculum frameworks of all states and territories and the national Statements of Learning for Science agreed to by all Australian jurisdictions in July 2006. The matrix was chosen so that the teachers in all states would be fully supported and their needs recognized. The matrix is organized using four conceptual science strands: Earth and Beyond, Energy and Change, Life and Living, and Natural and Processed Materials. The stages of learning are those developed for the national assessment of scientific literacy.

The unit topics for the matrix were chosen to build on students' natural curiosity and sense of wonder and to develop their passion for exploring how the world works. The titles are engaging for both students and teachers— for example, *Spinning in space, Water works, On the move, Plants in action,* and *Marvellous micro-organisms.*

173

In the classroom, science provides a meaningful context and a real purpose for learning literacy, and this relationship has been shown to be one of the most powerful outcomes of the project. Each Primary Connections unit includes a number of literacy skills to be developed during the unit. These include regular recordings of observations, labelled diagrams, tables of results, graphic representation of results, storyboards, accounts of interviews, and posters. The approach demonstrates the interdependence of science and literacy learning and gives students the opportunity to think about and represent their understanding of science as they inquire and report on their investigations.

A visit to classes participating in a unit of Primary Connections is highly rewarding. Students clearly respond to the day-to-day continuation of the investigations as they eagerly explore the topics. The teachers have pointed out that in addition to the science learning and the literacy learning, the participation of the students in the class contributes significantly to social skills and helps students learn the value of teamwork. The units also connect the learning of science to students' everyday lives and local communities.

174

THE IMPACT ON TEACHERS

The effect on teachers has also been very exciting. Teachers who have admitted that they did everything they could to avoid teaching science in their classes before their participation in Primary Connections are now excited about and proud of their ability to teach these units. The professional learning component of the program is central to assisting teachers in developing their confidence and competence in teaching science and literacy. The states and territories are adopting a range of ways to help teachers understand the underpinning ideas, such as how to help students undertake investigation and how to assess student learning.

In this program students need time to explore scientific phenomena before explanations are provided. For many teachers this is a very different and welcome way to teach science. However, they need time to rethink their teaching strategies. Centrally trained facilitators are key to implementing the program. By the end of 2008, several hundred of them from all states and territories will have undertaken three days of training to support schools to implement the program.

University educators who train future teachers must also be aware of the program. To this end representatives from every Australian university offering a course in primary science education attended a two-day workshop at the Academy's Shine Dome in Canberra—in itself a major achievement for the Academy and the Australian Department of Education, Science and Training, which provided funding for the workshop. 175

MAKING A DIFFERENCE

The Primary Connections program is an innovative package. It has been collaboratively developed and is based on sound philosophies. It is monitored by continuing research and evaluation and has undergone extensive trials in classrooms throughout Australia. One purpose of the program is to enhance the scientific literacy of our future communities. But mostly the aim is to excite teachers and equip them to teach science and to excite primary school students about science—to foster their love of learning. The evidence is that Primary Connections really is making a difference.

LET EVERY TONGUE SPEAK
AND EACH HEART FEEL

Carl Safina

I IMAGINE THAT THERE ARE SOME PRETTY SATISFIED people in other professions. I'd bet there are some people at ExxonMobil who are positively ecstatic about their multibillion-dollar profits. Well, maybe not ecstatic; people like that never seem happy. But satisfied with themselves, yes. I bet they are.

But who in the field of environment or conservation could seem satisfied? Since Aldo Leopold, since Rachel Carson—since Jesus for that matter—how many people who have preached peace and struggled for consideration of the wider world around us can feel that the future looks bright for children and other living things, that the world is increasingly secure, or that we have learned and applied our lessons well?

In the 1980s greed became trendy in the United States, and the United States—ever a trendsetter—helped set a worldwide tone. Conservation and the environment, while looking to me like increasingly urgent issues, nonetheless receded from public priorities. As bigger and bigger cars wasted more and more of the oil we had to drill harder and harder for, concern about the environment became positively unfashionable.

This development was partly the fault of environmentalists. Conservation often seemed to be presented as a contest or a dichotomy between people and nature: save a wetland/don't build homes; save trees/use less paper; save energy/drive less; save birds/don't use pesticides. It seemed that environmentalists were always asking people to do with less or to sacrifice—for the benefit of something else. Conservationists have long believed that we're all on the same ride, but we weren't communicating effectively.

In *The Outermost House*, Henry Beston famously wrote these resonant, elegant lines: "The animal shall not be measured by man. In a world older and more complete than ours they move finished and complete, gifted with extensions of the senses we have lost or never attained, living by voices we shall never hear. They are not brethren, they are not underlings; they are other nations, caught with ourselves in the net of life and time, fellow prisoners of the splendour and travail of the earth."

In one sense the entire conservation enterprise depends on getting people to understand that we are *all* caught in that same net, other living things and ourselves, everyone. And we'd best pay attention, because now the net might be of our own making.

THE WORLD ECONOMY has since the industrial revolution been based on an available, affordable, but inherently unsustainable energy source. One reason energy has been so cheap is that our economic system, with its prices and markets, has accounted for the benefits but excluded and ignored the damage to nature and life-support systems. Consequently, cognizant environmentalists seemed always to be wagging their fingers, scolding people, demanding sacrifice, saying the sky was falling.

What if the sky really is falling?

Climate change is likely to be the defining issue of the rest of our lives. It's not just a new environmental problem. In many ways it is a new *kind* of environmental problem. It draws a wider net than we've ever seen before. It tells us, with urgency and a clarity we have never before experienced, that we are indeed caught in that net, all fellow prisoners of our own ingenuity. What if we are all adrift aboard the same ark? What if we are just a living film on a blue and white marble in the black immensity of space?

From the climate problem, a new kind of environmentalism is emerging. The new environmentalism is running deeper and wider than before. And unlike many of our other environmental concerns, much of the climate issue is about not just our effect on other animals, not just bad consequences for birds, but the life-support capacity of the whole planet, including people and the things that support human civilization, such as agriculture and cities. After losing market share for two decades, we environmentalists seem to have turned a corner, as concern

179

about the environment is gaining a kind of momentum not seen since the 1970s.

Rachel Carson's *Silent Spring* drew the whole world together for the first time. She showed that toxic chemicals posed wide, unexpected threats to many living things, including people. Although her main focus was on wildlife—what if it was spring, and no birds sang?—some of the greatest strides in the early years of the environmental movement derived from the perception that harming our environment was largely a human health issue. It's likely that a lot of the cancers people suffer are related to human-made toxic chemicals, but the links are unclear because people are exposed to so many things for many years. Although chemicals cause animal cancers in controlled laboratory experiments, the chemical threat is not obvious in our daily lives. You can't see it or smell it or taste it. It's not visceral.

Climate change is different. It's the biggest umbrella issue of our lives, overshadowing everything. It would be difficult to imagine a bigger chronic issue. (Catastrophic nuclear war would be worse, but it won't be the result of everyone's day-to-day living, and every sane human wants to avoid nuclear holocaust.) To run our whole civilization, we've created a peaceful, productive engine that just happens to be weakening the planet's life-support systems. How can we extricate ourselves now?

Climate change is proving to be a great community maker because it involves everyone and everything.

And it's a great accounting reformer. Because economic systems have been happy to internalize profits and determined to ignore environmental costs, global warming may turn out to be the greatest accounting and market failure of all time. But climate change promises to send us the bill, in the form of storms, floods, refugees, crop failure, pests, spreading diseases. And now markets are responding. Where I live, on Long Island, New York, several major insurance companies will no longer write new home insurance policies. They're afraid of the massive losses they predict will come from rises in sea level and intensified storm surges fueled by warming.

One conceptual tunnel out of the climate crisis is that while civilization is addicted to fossil fuels, no one actually *wants* to use fossil fuels. What we *want* is for our cars to go, our refrigerators to be cold, and our water to be heated. We don't care *how* we get those things. And so if we can avoid getting those things in bad ways, and learn how to get them in good ways, we'll be satisfied and we'll never miss oil and coal. That may seem so simplistic as to sound almost meaningless. But it makes the difference between calls for more oil, more coal, more conventional power plants on the one hand, and more efficiency, more energy options, less energy centralization, more energy independence on the other

Another new thing is that some mainstream businesses, including some of the international giants, are increasingly going green. And they're doing so for various reasons. They're saving money by becoming more efficient. They're preparing for oil shocks by going to sustainable sources. They're looking for a market edge with good PR. Some even seem to be making these changes because they're trying to do the right thing.

We are really starting to see, in a new way, that we are all connected. And unlike pesticides, climate change is not just bad for birds but even *worse* for crops. Climate change helps erase that false people-versus-nature dichotomy. And the climate is more tangible than toxic chemicals: people can feel the heat. The hot air is breathing down our necks in a way we've never experienced with any other issue of conservation and the environment.

BUT THIS NEW turn is just beginning. We have a very long way to go. The public will have to support major efforts in research and technology. To avert catastrophic problems will require that millions of people understand things in new ways. We will have to find new technical and social solutions and convey new ethical meaning.

So we must ask: why has it taken so long for people to respond to this issue? We've known for decades that we need new sources of energy. In fact, all the environmental issues of today have been discussed my whole adult life. In junior high school, I learned that pesticides and other chemicals could harm the health of humans and nontarget wildlife. We understood that the human population was exploding. During the 1970s, as boats from Eastern Europe and the former Soviet Union began taking vast quantities of fish off our coasts, I learned that we could deplete the seas. I learned that oil was limited and that it caused us to harm wildlife habitats and rely on unsavory governments. I learned about how much energy and money we could save by driving smaller, high-mileage cars. I learned that carbon dioxide could intensify the "greenhouse effect" and change the climate. Despite knowing these things more than thirty years ago—and especially in the last twenty years—it seems we did next to nothing. So the problems of those times have become the crises of today.

Why didn't we act more effectively on all this information? Why does it always seem that people are so unmoved, for so long, on matters of great urgency? Great challenges face us, so we need to understand what to do differently, what lessons we must learn.

MY LIFE HAS been intertwined with nature and conservation from childhood. Most of my interests and work have involved wildlife, especially fish and other ocean wildlife. I got involved professionally in conservation because I could see ocean wildlife populations declining.

I've always believed that environmental and conservation concerns were correct and that as we learned more about the threats, people would realize that what they held dear was at risk. That's partly because I have a scientific mind and I'm persuaded by data. It's also because I love nature and find the living world miraculous, and so the risks scare me.

When I began working to improve public policies, as a scientist I assumed we lacked the information we needed to make wise decisions. But I quickly realized that we had all the information we needed to do the right things. Yet even though we had plenty of information, public policies lagged far behind the information. I could not understand why.

Here is what I have come to believe: information abounds, but information alone does not move most people, because information alone does not change values.

Conservationists, who after all are inspired to work in conservation not just because of information they have but because of how it makes them *feel*, need to find better ways to fuse scientific information with a wider array of human values, including those powerful values arising from religious tradition. The goal: to *inspire* (rather than argue for) a new orientation toward conservation, nature, and environment, an orientation that is value based and draws on the call to compassion and stewardship.

Getting anywhere requires both a destination and navigational equipment. Factual findings can suggest the destination. Values are the moral compass.

Information changes. Values last lifetimes. Values determine how new information will be incorporated into living. But rather than try to change values, we might be much more effective if we found ways to work within people's existing values framework. The trick, I think, is not to say, "Here is some new information that should change your values." I believe that science and conservation must be communicated not just through information and statistics but also through value-based channels of understanding, such as story, personal experience, metaphor, and song. Those who have important information to communicate must find the channels that are open in their intended audience.

Other such channels include allegory, anecdote, image, community, ceremony, theater, faith. Think of it as a question of *translation*. Or think of it this way: we have to try every key we have in our effort to unlock each heart.

The challenge is to get people to open up to new factual information. Because most people are mainly motivated by values, we must communicate in ways that allow people to receive and assimilate messages within their existing moral and ethical context. In this way they feel a self-generated call to act.

We must deal with information, also, because information tells us how the world is changing. But we must focus on communicating through and about values, because compared with information, values are deeper and longer lasting.

This is not a matter of manipulating people; it's a matter of communicating matters of the utmost importance to the future of life. Science needs a human face. We need to increasingly focus on formulating messages that allow people to recognize themselves.

Because we are talking about health and the ability of our planet to continue supporting life, formulating such messages should be possible. There has never been a more important time to take a new approach to communicating. Given what is at stake, any new communication efforts must aim to build new audiences outside the choir.

The sea has been my vehicle, but what we are really talking about is hope. Hope is the sense that things can really be made better. Hope can motivate the many caring people who are sitting on the sidelines waiting to feel inspired to believe that their efforts might actually matter. Rather than fixating on the negative, we all need to focus on how we can help create change through our daily and collective activities. We must give people ways to think differently and to see themselves and the world in new contexts. And we must allow people to envision new ways to act.

Science, conservation, and nature have had only a few great public translators. Those few luminaries have lit the path. They've shown the importance of being scientifically and intellectually rigorous *and* recognizing that science without communication has no value.

So let this be their legacy: more translators, more communicators, more people who can show other people that we are all caught in the same net, who can show that what they care about is what we all really care about.

TRAVELS with

DAVID SUZUKI

So here in the last part of my life,

I can only hope that from an elder's

perspective, I can offer a bit of clichéd advice.

Slow down and smell the roses. Recognize

that we live in a world where everything

is connected to everything else and so whatever

we do has repercussions. There is a tomorrow

and what we do now will influence what tomorrow

we arrive at. We owe it to future generations

to think about them before leaping ahead.

{ DAVID SUZUKI }

THE GEOGRAPHY OF HOPE

——— *Thomas Berger* ———

WHEN DAVID SUZUKI AND THE *Nature of Things*
asked me to return to the Mackenzie Valley in the summer of 2005, it was an opportunity to visit people and
places that I first got to know in the 1970s as commissioner of the Mackenzie Valley Pipeline Inquiry.

In 1977, after two and a half years of hearings, in
my report entitled "Northern Frontier, Northern Homeland," I recommended that no pipeline be built until land
claims had been settled and measures taken to protect
critical habitat. Since then the settlement of land claims
has made the Dene and the Inuvialuit the owners of hundreds of thousands of hectares of land, including surface
and subsurface resources, and has provided guarantees of
their right to hunt, fish, and trap. The land claims settle-
ments have also provided for setting aside protected areas

for caribou, migratory birds, and other species. More-over, the Dene and the Inuvialuit are important players in working out the choices that face the region. They will have an influential—if not decisive—voice in determin-ing whether a Mackenzie Valley gas pipeline is to be built today. They are no longer spectators in their own drama.

The question facing the peoples of the Mackenzie Valley today is, of course, still about the pipeline. A joint review panel is considering the impact of the pipeline, and then the pipeline issue will go to the National Energy Board. But it is not the same pipeline that I dealt with thirty years ago.

IN 1974 THE pipeline was to bring natural gas from Prud-hoe Bay along the north slope of Alaska and across the Arctic coast of the Yukon to the Mackenzie Delta, where it would pick up Canadian gas and then carry the gas from both frontiers through the valley to Alberta. Today's Mackenzie Valley pipeline runs along an all-Canadian route, however, carrying gas from the three fields in the Mackenzie Delta to Alberta.

The reason is that thirty years ago Canada decided there should not be a pipeline across the northern Yukon. In the 1970s the Inuvialuit and the Gwich'in argued that a pipeline along the Arctic coast from Prudhoe Bay would drive the Porcupine caribou herd from their calv-ing grounds along the coastal plain. The case they made was altogether convincing. I recommended that critical

190

habitat along the Arctic coast of the Yukon extending south to Old Crow be set aside as wilderness to protect the calving grounds of the Porcupine caribou herd (today 125,000 caribou) and the staging area for 500,000 snow geese. The Aboriginal peoples would retain the right to live, hunt, fish, and trap within the park and, together with Parks Canada, would manage the park.

In 1977 the gas pipeline project depended upon the route along the Arctic coast of the Yukon. If there were no pipeline across the Yukon, there could be no pipeline from Prudhoe Bay in Alaska. The project would be at an end.

And that is how it turned out; no pipeline was to cross the calving grounds, no pipeline was to bring gas from Prudhoe Bay, and no pipeline would be built along the Mackenzie Valley until land claims were settled.

The Inuvialuit and the Gwich'in provided in their land claims agreements for the establishment of two wilderness parks, Ivvavik, to protect the Yukon coastal plain, and Vuntut, to protect the lands extending south to Old Crow on the Porcupine River, for the protection of the caribou and the snow geese.

In my report I also urged the United States to protect the contiguous areas of Alaska, where the calving grounds of the Porcupine herd are more extensive than in Canada. I went to Washington, DC, in 1978 to testify before Senate and House committees to argue for international cooperation in protecting the herd. Those were the days of the Carter administration, and I received a sympathetic hearing. The United States established the Arctic National Wildlife Refuge. Canada signed a treaty with the United States to protect the caribou calving grounds on both sides of the international boundary. Today, however, the Bush administration wants to drill for oil in the calving grounds on the Alaska side.

On our trip that summer of 2005 with David and *The Nature of Things*, we camped in the refuge as the herd was leaving the calving grounds on the coast and beginning its migration back into the mountains. We could see them in their thousands on the slopes, and sometimes, with their calves, they came very near to the creek where we had pitched our tents. It was solemn, stunning, and stirring. To the Gwich'in this is a sacred place. And so it should be to all of us.

The idea of drilling for oil and gas in the calving grounds represents a kind of technological manifest destiny, and it represents a risk to the caribou.

In 1637 Descartes predicted that man's reason and knowledge would enable us "to render ourselves the lords and possessors of nature." The advance of science and technology has brought us very close to achieving this state. In fact we tend to think of the history of the last four hundred years as the history of the triumph throughout the world of Western science and technology. We used to think that the changes wrought by science and technology would be altogether benign, that science and technology could provide the means to abolish human misery. For many this belief is still the secular faith of our time. In recent years, however, another view has begun to take hold: that the advance of science and technology—especially large-scale technology—may entail social, economic, and environmental consequences whose costs may be enormous and that may condition, or even severely limit, the choices open to us in the future. The advent of global warming has forced millions to consider such consequences and the choices that may be forced upon us.

Industrialism not only creates wealth but also shatters established social systems and is a powerful instrument of control in the new social systems to which it gives rise. Its attraction lies both in the affluence it promises and in the freedom it offers from the constraints imposed by nature and tradition. Because industrialism emphasizes material values and challenges an ethically oriented idea of society, many oppose its proliferation.

Two ways of looking at the world are in conflict, as they have always been. Throughout the New World, since the time of Cortez and Pizarro, people have sought wealth at the frontier, wealth to enrich the metropolis. Ever since the days of New Spain, human beings have wished for another Montezuma's treasure, another Atahualpa to be ransomed. The drive to extract the wealth of the New World continues today. But now it is intensified by the instrumentalities of modem industrialism, in which the predominant place of large-scale, capital-intensive technology is assumed. Our notions of progress have acquired a technological and industrial definition.

But another strain has always run through our attitude toward the land and its resources. It is exemplified by the members of the first European settlement in North America (north of Florida)—the Frenchmen who established Port Royal on the Bay of Fundy in 1605. One of them, Marc Lescarbot, a lawyer from Paris, wrote in his diary:

> . . . farming must be our goal. That is the first mine for which we must search. And it is better worth than the treasures of Atahualpa for whoso has corn, wine, cattle, linen, cloth, leather, iron and lastly, codfish, need have naught to do with treasure.

It is not surprising that these settlers—who came to be known as the Acadians—had the most harmonious relations of any European settlers with the Aboriginal peoples of North America. The view of human occupation of the land that they exemplified is one that has an increasing number of adherents today in Canada.

In North America a particular idea of progress has become fixed in our consciousness, but North Americans also have a strong identification with the values of the wilderness and of the land itself, a deeply felt concern for the environment. In Canada this concern goes back a long way. It was John A. Macdonald who, in 1885, the very year that the construction of the Canadian Pacific

Railway was completed, brought a bill before the House of Commons to establish Rocky Mountain (now Banff) National Park, Canada's first national park. In recent years we have seen the growth of ecological awareness, a growing concern for wilderness and wildlife, and environmental legislation that parallels—although it does not match—the increasing spread of our technology and the consumption of natural resources.

I do not urge that we seek to turn back the clock, to return in some way to nature, or even to deplore, in a high-minded and sentimental manner, the real achievements of the industrial system. Rather we must realize that environmental values constitute an invaluable aspect of modern-day life: the observance of environmental values is a contribution to, not a repudiation of, the civilization upon which we depend.

It may be said that this is all very well in the case of urban amenities, recreation areas, campgrounds, and national parks. But of what use is a far-off landscape or seascape that urban dwellers may never see? Why should it matter to the urbanite whether or not the Porcupine caribou herd still makes its annual journey to the Arctic coast, whether or not the white whales abounding in Canadian waters along the Arctic Coast and Hudson Bay maintain their present numbers, and whether or not the snow geese still feed on the islands of the Arctic Archipelago? I think it matters because wilderness and wildlife are essential to a sense of order in the universe. They affirm a deeply felt need to comprehend the wholeness of nature and of life. They offer serenity and peace of mind. As Wallace Stegner wrote:

> Without any remaining wilderness we are committed . . . to a headlong drive into our technological termite-life, the Brave New World of a completely man-controlled environment . . . We simply need that wild country . . . [as] part of the geography of hope.

In Canada the policy has been to expand our industrial machine to the limit of our country's frontiers. It is natural for us to think of developing the frontier, of subduing the land, populating it with people from the metropolitan centers, and extracting its resources to fuel our industry and heat our homes. We have never had to consider the uses of restraint. The question that the rise in the Earth's temperature, itself owing to the triumph of industrialism, requires us to face is this: are we serious people, willing and able to make up our own minds, or are we simply driven, by technology and egregious patterns of consumption, to deplete our resources wherever and whenever we find them? Can we—and others—turn away from this monolithic economic mode?

David Suzuki has been urging us for decades to consider an alternative to industrialism, not just to preserve wildlife and wilderness, but to preserve other species, from insects in the Amazon to polar bears in the Arctic.

196

His campaign in support of an alternative ethic of development has made an enormous difference. His prescient warnings of climate change, of the recklessness of our present approach, are now lodged in the minds of Canadians.

The intellectual challenge of comprehending the shape of the postindustrial world, of comprehending the moral, social, and economic goals that will inform that era, now faces us all.

EARLY YEARS
WITH DAVID SUZUKI

John Lucchesi

I FIRST MET DAVID SUZUKI IN 1964. HAD THE PLAN-
ets been aligned somewhat differently, we would have
met earlier. Following his undergraduate years at
Amherst College, David wanted to work toward a PhD at
the University of California–Berkeley; for some reason,
his application was not processed, and in 1958 he landed
at the University of Chicago. At the same time, I had
applied to both universities to work with the very same
professors; unlike David, I opted to go to Berkeley.

When we did finally meet, David had left his first aca-
demic position at the University of Alberta to start his
career at the University of British Columbia; I was in my
second postdoctoral year at the University of Oregon in
Ed Novitski's laboratory. On special occasions, when a
speaker of note would be scheduled to visit the genetics

department at the University of Washington, Novitski would send us to Seattle to attend the seminar. On one particular occasion, James Crow—a well-known geneticist from the University of Wisconsin—had been invited to deliver a lecture.

The opportunity to meet Jim Crow and to hear him lecture was as attractive to us as it was to David, who traveled south with his students for that same purpose. There was another postdoctoral fellow in Novitski's laboratory— Jim Peacock, an exceptionally bright Australian who had studied plant cytogenetics for his doctorate and had come to Eugene to learn chromosome mechanics under the tutelage of a master of the field. Following Crow's seminar Jim Peacock and I met David at an informal reception and the seeds of a great scientific relationship, later to become a deep and wonderful friendship, were planted.

A few months later, David came to Eugene, where once again he, Jim Peacock, and I had long scientific discussions. I remember that David asked Jim whether he would consider applying for a position at UBC. Jim had his eye on loftier venues, and when the appropriate opportunities did not develop in the United States, he returned to Australia, where eventually he became Director of the Division of Plant Industries at the Commonwealth Scientific and Industrial Research Organization in Canberra.

I confess that I was chagrined by David's attempts to recruit Peacock while ignoring the fact that I too would soon be on the job market. All was forgiven when—in

1967, two years after my appointment as an assistant professor at the University of North Carolina in Chapel Hill—Dave (please note the subtle change in how I refer to him) asked me to teach a summer version of the genetics course that he had developed and to spend the rest of my time in his lab.

That summer was one of the great professional and personal experiences of my career. Dave had assembled a group of amazingly dedicated students who shared his passion for scientific research. His energy and magnetism attracted all of us like proverbial moths to the light, and in turn he fed on our excitement. We talked interminably about the burning scientific questions of the day; we spent hours devising complicated, clever experimental strategies; we ate together, fished together, camped together, listened to the Animals, the Beatles, Credence Clearwater Revival, Gordon Lightfoot, the Mamas and the Papas (sure, we smoked some weed together, but of course we never inhaled!).

The field of genetics, and indeed all of biology, had passed through the most significant landmarks since the rediscovery of Mendel's laws and the identification of DNA as the genetic material: the resolution of the structure of DNA and the use of bacteria and their viruses as experimental tools. *Drosophila* had emerged as the primary-model organism for the study of the properties of chromosomes as vehicles for the transmission of genetic information. We all hoped to be able to connect the dots—to understand the molecular basis for the transmission of genes and for their functions. The ultimate goal for many of us was to get at cellular differentiation and organismal development. It was abundantly clear that the blueprint for all biological properties and functions was the genetic material; we had become geneticists in order to understand the properties of the blueprint and how the information it contained is extracted and used to make cells, tissues, and whole living organisms. David was interested, as we all were, in the behavior of chromosomes during cell division and gamete formation, and his lab was contributing to the body of knowledge that we called chromosome mechanics. It was this phase of his research that led to the one paper that we published together.

But David's genius was to realize that some of the tools developed by microbial geneticists could be applied to study complex developmental pathways and functions in multicellular model organisms such as fruitflies. One of these tools was the conditional mutation—a change in a gene that would lead to a loss of its function under the influence of some particular environmental conditions. For example, a gene with a conditional mutation may not function if the organism that carries it is raised at high ambient temperature but would function normally if the organism is maintained at lower temperatures. By raising mutant organisms at lower temperatures and later switching them to a higher temperature, one could study in adults the effects of mutations that would normally lead to death very early in development. David's lab was the first not only to show that conditional mutations could be induced and selected in *Drosophila* but also to show that such mutations could be used to study the genetic basis of complex traits and physiological pathways such as muscle function and behavior.

Soon after my return to Chapel Hill, I received a letter from the head of the department, asking if I would be interested in a faculty position at UBC. This offer caused me to sink into the depths of a deep dilemma, rivaled only by the one I experienced several years later following the offer of the chair of the genetics department at UC–Berkeley (I accepted that offer and then declined it two agonizing days later; but that is another story).

A job in Canada meant immigrating to a new country from one into which I had immigrated only a few years earlier. But wouldn't the effort be worthwhile, given the marvelous scientific environment offered by the Suzuki lab, where I had spent such a wonderful three months?

As it turns out, all of the characteristics that I admired and loved in David eventually led to my decision not to pursue the possibility of a move: he had such a magnetic personality and was so talented and focused that it would be very hard for me to stay intellectually and professionally independent. To achieve independence I would have to compete with David, and that would be both a distasteful and a losing proposition. One could say that because I so admired and liked David, I decided not to become one of his colleagues.

Three years later I returned to UBC for the summer. This time I had no teaching duties, and I planned to spend all of my time in David's lab. His students and post-doctoral fellows were among the best of their generation, and most went on to highly successful careers. Although the level of the research was better than ever, the atmosphere had changed: from a scientific Shangri-La, the lab had become a high-powered, highly competitive venue like many in the United States.

The main reason for the change was that David himself was undergoing a philosophical transmutation. His all-encompassing belief that science is the core of human existence and that research is the endeavor that most defines our humanness was tempered, if not challenged, by concerns about the consequences of scientific discoveries and the social responsibilities of the discoverers. This new frame of mind led him to wonder how the famous scientists of the time felt and, eventually, to formalize their responses into a series of interviews that were broadcast by the CBC on a program entitled *Suzuki on Science*.

I have often wondered what transformed David, the concerned geneticist, into one of the most passionate, dedicated, popular, and therefore effective advocates for respect and solicitude toward our planet's environments. As most scientists would, I have a hypothesis. The seed was planted by the scientific breakthrough that the new technology of genetic cloning represented. This technology opened up a Pandora's box of scenarios ranging from the total abolition of the human race by some uncontrollable infectious agent to the creation of superhumans through genetic engineering. All of these possibilities were terrifying to everyone, with the exception of the scientists who were developing ways of using genetic cloning to answer basic scientific questions, questions that had been out of their reach but that they might now have a chance to address. Research in molecular biology and molecular genetics required an ever-increasing level of funding; to secure the necessary financial support, scientists touted the many useful applications of gene cloning, exaggerating both their imminence and their power.

Somewhere along the line, David became as concerned about the pervasive illusion that science could reverse or prevent all of the harmful consequences of the industrial revolution and its periodic reincarnation as he had been about the perils of human genetic engineering. Because of his scientific background and his gift for proselytizing, he chose to act on this concern. When David found this new career, science lost one of its most talented practitioners, and our Big Blue Marble gained one of its most fervent defenders.

THE WONDER OF THE
NATURAL WORLD

—— *Robyn Williams* ——

IN AUGUST 1975 I WAS ON MY FIRST TRIP TO NORTH
America. I had often dreamed about this legendary continent, picturing a combination of Shangri-La and the
Black Hole of Calcutta. It turned out I was right. From
the Bowery in New York to the flashy villas of La Jolla,
from the flat scrub and brutal turnpikes of Houston to
the grand, leafy vistas of Vancouver, I was astounded by
the contrasts.

It was in Vancouver that my broadcasting career really
took off. I had been playing with radio since 1972, covering the last two *Apollo* missions to the moon (16 and
17), presenting a few experimental science programs on
the ABC (Australian Broadcasting Commission, as it then
was), and having fun without real commitment. I did
not expect to stay long in Sydney, as I had grown up in

Europe and thought I would return there. Yet something was changing in the world, something momentous was happening, and as I made yet more programs, I began to sense that it was worth being part of that transformation.

Apollo had given us that thrilling, exquisite, historic photograph of the blue Earth hanging alone in the dark sky, showing both the beauty and the limits of our celestial home. For the first time, we could *see* our world was finite. Then came Stockholm 1972; the UN Conference on the Environment, the first of many over the years in different parts of the world, marked the start of a global awareness of a green challenge. At the same time, the Club of Rome and *Limits to Growth* marked a brave attempt to discover the boundaries of our human empire, how far we could expand into natural surroundings we had always assumed went on forever.

Three years later, with a brief stop in Palo Alto to see my old friend Paul Ehrlich, who had sounded the alarm with *The Population Bomb* in 1968, I arrived in Vancouver. It was spectacular. I had heard the legend, but nothing had prepared me for the immensity of the bay, with its vast, forested mountains, for the water and the bridges, or for the superb Stanley Park in the middle of town, around which I have run now scores of times. How miserable it was to hear thirty-two years later of the ferocious storm that had smashed so many of the trees in this precious plot of urban green.

I was in Canada to attend the Congress of the Pacific Science Association. It was to be held at the University of

British Columbia, the high campus to which over eight thousand delegates would fly. Some were famous, like Thor Heyerdahl, the explorer, and Herman Kahn, the futurologist. Others were working scientists trying to put their research into a global context with an emphasis on the Pacific: anthropologists, geographers, archaeologists, marine biologists, economists (it was an ecumenical gathering), and a few journos.

I fell in with the guys from the CBC. My mission was to record (on my own) a one-hour program called *The Science Show,* which would be squirted through the satellite to Australia. I did not realize at the time that this would be the first of many hundreds of *Science Shows* I would assemble every week to this very day thirty-three years later. Nor did I realize that, across the UBC campus from where we were based in that August summer of 1975, was a guy in the genetics department called Suzuki who would be doing much the same thing with a show called *Quirks and Quarks* for the CBC. Both programs would be an hour long (both 53 minutes and 55 seconds, actually), both on Saturdays at the same time (noon), both repeated on Monday evening, and both with a remit to look at science in a new way, as if it were a truly human activity with consequences far beyond the scrubbed walls and black-box apparatus of high-tech labs. Coincidence or co-evolution?

I made my program. It featured the energy crisis (with Lord Ritchie Calder from the UK), the future of nuclear power and the disaffection of youth with science (with

Gerard Piel, publisher of *Scientific American*), the arms race (with Herman Kahn of the Hudson Institute) and the passage of Polynesians from the east and South America to populate the Pacific Islands (Thor Heyerdahl). Climate change too, would you believe, also came up. Over thirty years ago, some of the main quandaries that now consume us were already obvious.

David Suzuki—though I knew nothing about him in 1975—would also follow these concerns, now as a journalist rather than as a professor.

We did meet, ten years later. It was in Toronto, where David had just wrapped an edition of *The Nature of Things* for CBC-TV, and we met in the pub. Dave still enjoyed a beer back then, as I do now, and we talked all evening. He was more one of the gang, jokey and relaxed—not the slightly withdrawn pundit he's become since. I was involved with the new Commission for the Future in Australia, and I invited David to come south as our guest.

"They won't like the kinds of things I say," he warned me cheerfully. "That's fine," I responded, "Australia needs a shake-up." And that's what duly happened. He came; he spoke; I recorded his speeches and put him on *The Science Show* many times. Within just a few months, David Suzuki was a national figure in Australia, as he is in Canada. He has been back to see us every year since.

What happened? Why would a Canadian genetics prof with a flair for radio and TV become a household name on the other side of the planet? Yes, he speaks superbly,

208

with that rich maple syrup voice and those wonderfully expressive hands—but there are plenty of orators on the environment. He uses narrative and imagery like no other, and despite being a Canadian, even manages the odd jest. That, however, is not enough to create twenty years of packed houses.

For me the clue is his uncompromising intensity. Suzuki doesn't swerve. This is not a man given to easy, pleasant compromise. He lays things on the line. Relentlessly. And he has been proved right. Whereas in the mid-1980s, many of us were maligned as Maoist insurgents plotting to undermine capitalism and the American (Australian/Canadian) way of life, we now worry that we *understated* the problem. As I look back, it is almost ludicrous recalling the lengths to which some commentators were willing to go to infer conspiracies. They called us watermelons—green on the outside, red within. Cryptic Commies. "Moaning Minnies" was Margaret Thatcher's take. In Australia in the 1970s, our groundbreaking reports on the dangers of asbestos, lead in petrol, Minimata disease, involving mercury both in Japan and among Native Americans, were attacked; even our warnings about tobacco were identified as gross examples of leftist bias.

Once, at an American Association for the Advancement of Science (AAAS) press conference on climate, I was sitting next to a posh, beetle-browed, rather twitchy writer from a British newspaper, based in London. We were looking at the panel of three scientists waiting

209

to address the packed room. "Robyn," whispered the intrepid correspondent from the "*Torygraph*," hiding his mouth behind his hand as if making a connection with MI5 on the streets of Moscow, "are they all commies?"

The topics to be addressed were ozone depletion and greenhouse gasses (clearly suspect!), so I leaned over to the interlocutor and breathed, "You're spot on. How did you know? The one on the left is Professor Sherwood Rowland, who won the Nobel Prize in Chemistry and is a past president of AAAS. Brilliant cover! The one in the middle is from MIT—a campus well known for harboring moles like Chomsky. That's Professor Mario Molina; he's also got a Nobel Prize. And the third is the CEO of an Ivy League university. All brilliant disguises, but pinkos every one." Mr. Scoop nodded keenly and wrote down all the tripe I had been putting in his ear as fast as he could. Then I thought it funny; now I think it is sad.

All that time wasted. David Suzuki was on message from the start. On the Amazon, on fisheries, on climate, on our connections with nature, and on the future, but it takes more than a generation to get a majority of people to realize that they must act.

Inevitably, we disagree on a few topics. I am less impressed than he is by the way some indigenous folk have looked after their natural heritage. You need only visit New Zealand, where the giant moa and kakapo flourished just eight hundred years ago, when people first arrived, and are now virtually extinct (though the kakapo clings on with around-the-clock protection), or read Jared Diamond's *Collapse* to see that humans can sometimes be lousy stewards. I am also certainly bothered by the *politics* of genetic modification (GM) but see little evidence in the science of it to match concerns in other environmental areas. I believe it is as counterproductive to be universally suspicious of an entire field like GM as it was for Greenpeace to want to condemn the element chlorine (!) as a chemical worthy of banning. I also see science as more of an instrument of hope than David does, often likening it, as he has, to a narrow, reductionist part of establishment myopia.

We all have our blind spots. Paul Ehrlich was once a member of the American Republican Party (he resigned in protest when the ex-drunk, failed captain of industry G.W. Bush became president). E.O. Wilson did not fully understand the impact of his sociobiology, Jared Diamond has a very broad brush with history, and Rachel Carson may not have noticed the usefulness of DDT in some limited circumstances. But we're also all inconvertibly human.

Well, here we are, only just into the twenty-first century, and the warnings we gave thirty or forty years ago are terrifyingly confirmed. A more acid ocean absorbing carbon dioxide to give carbonic acid could dissolve coral reefs by 2065. The heating of the atmosphere will be greater than we feared, and positive feedback is likely. The fish in the seas have been reduced by 90 percent in the past twenty years. The great apes could be gone in a generation and with them most tigers, not to mention less iconic and conspicuous species.

Meanwhile, we continue to indulge in the greatest binge since the gormandizing fat man in *Monty Python* blew up. American households throw away US$48.3 billion dollars' worth of food each year (the total, including stores and hotels, is $120 billion); the cost of traffic jams in the United States is US$100 billion a year; the number of bottles used for water thrown away in the United States every three weeks would reach to the moon. You know the numbers. There are plenty more like that. It is grotesque.

Tim Jones is a Western Cherokee working as a professor of anthropology at the University of Arizona in Tucson. It is he who published the figures on food waste. I ask him what it is that makes folk willing to be so appallingly profligate, knowing, as they must, that we have an environmental disaster looming and food is a key part of the problem.

Tim replies that people no longer know where food comes from. It is not linked to nature anymore. It's just there on the shelf. What do we do about it, I ask. He has two suggestions. The first is that our tiny kids must grow their own lunch at school, watch the plants come up, nurture and then harvest them. The second is that they should visit the local abattoir and see their dinner being prepared to die. It won't be nice, but it will be very edifying. The experience may also change what's on their menu.

The hope is that measures like these can have a tremendous impact. Cities like London are four times as wasteful of energy as they need be. Big cities could reorganize their buildings today and cut their bills massively. A friend of mine who does audits of offices for big business promises a saving of 30 to 40 percent almost immediately. That is even before the auditors look at traffic, the other huge energy cost in cities. Why do 72 percent of Sydney-siders commute by car? What allows these bloated Prada-wrapped wasters to sit in solitary splendid isolation (few of them share) as part of that daily, predictable gridlock, while the rest of us pay two bucks on the bus? Why are executives given cars as part of their packages? It's like giving cartons of cigarettes for Christmas. Or offering kids a fourth helping of ice cream and cake. But the point is that the leeway for amelioration is huge.

And we can turn around many aspects of modern life quickly, if society is willing. One measure, long overdue, is to make public transport free. Most of the charges are swallowed by fare collection anyway.

Is there time? Yes, there is, I think to myself on Monday, Wednesday, and Friday. The rest of the week, I'm not so sure. When I last saw David Suzuki, we exchanged a few bleak concerns about the world's prospects. It is touch and go. And I suspect neither Dave nor I will be witness to the outcome. A mixed blessing!

And yet... if there is one thing, apart from what we leave for our children, that makes catastrophe unthinkable, it is the wonder of the natural world. David Suzuki, when he is not talking green, is devoted to those mountains, the fish in the streams, the bears in the forest, and even those once-mysterious genes and molecules now revealed in cells. It is all so exquisite and remarkable. By 2009 we will have known about these genes and molecules, the driving force of nature, for a mere 150 years, the time elapsed since Charles Darwin published *Origin of Species*. Our global concern about the environment, which really took off in 1972, is barely half the lifetime of the average Canadian man or woman. We have barely begun, and yet we now face our greatest challenge.

Time to get moving.

AUTHOR BIOGRAPHIES

RICK BASS is the author of twenty-three books of fiction and nonfiction, including, most recently, a story collection, *The Lives of Rocks*, which was a finalist for the Story Prize and was chosen as a Best Book of the Year by the *Rocky Mountain News*. His first short story collection, *The Watch*, won the PEN/Nelson Algren Award, and his 2002 collection *The Hermit's Story* was a *Los Angeles Times* Best Book of the Year. Bass's stories have also been awarded the Pushcart Prize and the O. Henry Award and have been collected in *The Best American Short Stories*. He lives with his family in northwest Montana's Yaak Valley, where he is active with a local place-based conservation organization, the Yaak Valley Forest Council (www.yaakvalley.org), which is working to designate the last roadless lands in the Yaak as permanently protected wilderness.

THOMAS BERGER was appointed to the Supreme Court of British Columbia in 1971 and served on the bench until 1983. He has worked hard to ensure that development on Aboriginal people's land has resulted in benefits to those indigenous people and is best known for his work as Commissioner of the Mackenzie Valley Pipeline Inquiry. The report he prepared for that inquiry, *Northern Frontier, Northern Homeland*, sold more copies than any other federal government publication. Berger's memoir, *One Man's Justice: A Life in the Law,* spans forty years of precedent-making cases and includes the landmark case of Calder v. British Columbia, during which he asserted that Aboriginal rights have a distinct place in Canadian law. Berger's success in the Calder case laid the foundation upon which most modern treaty-making cases are argued. He is the author of *Village Journey, Fragile Freedoms: Human Rights and Dissent in Canada,* and *A Long and Terrible Shadow.* He is an Officer of the Order of Canada and a member of the Order of British Columbia.

SHARON BUTALA is an award-winning and bestselling author of sixteen books, both fiction and nonfiction; she has produced five plays, won magazine awards, and published poetry and essays. Her classic *The Perfection of the Morning* was a finalist for the Governor General's Award, as was the story collection *Queen of the Headaches; Fever,* another story collection, which won the 1992 Authors' Award for Paperback Fiction and was shortlisted for the Commonwealth Writers' Award. *Lilac Moon: Dreaming of the Real West* won the Saskatchewan Book Award. Butala is a recipient of the Marian Engel Award and is an Officer of the Order of Canada. She lives near Eastend, Saskatchewan, where she helped to establish Wallace Stegner House, a valued retreat for artists. In 1996 Sharon and her husband, Peter, turned their ranch over to The Nature Conservancy of Canada to establish the Old Man On His Back Prairie and Heritage Conservation Area.

216

DR. HELEN CALDICOTT is the world's leading spokesperson for the antinuclear movement, the cofounder of Physicians for Social Responsibility, a nominee for the Nobel Peace Prize, and the 2003 winner of the Lannan Cultural Freedom Prize. Trained as a physician, and—after four decades of antinuclear activism—thoroughly versed in the science of nuclear energy, she is the bestselling author of *Nuclear Madness* and *Missile Envy*; her most recent book is *Nuclear Power Is Not the Answer*. She divides her time between Australia and Washington, DC, where she recently established the Nuclear Policy Research Institute.

DR. ADRIAN FORSYTH is Vice President for Programs at Blue Moon Fund (www.bluemoonfund.org), an organization that supports new economic, cultural, and environmental approaches to resource use, energy use, and urban development. He previously worked as Director of Biodiversity Science for the Andes/Amazon at the Gordon and Betty Moore Foundation. He received his PhD in tropical ecology from Harvard University and has worked as Vice President of Conservation International. He is currently a research associate at the Smithsonian Institution, and serves as President of the Board of the Amazon Conservation Association, USA. He is the author of nine books, including: *Tropical Nature*, *Mammals of the Canadian Wild*, *The Natural History of Sex*, *The Nature of Birds*, *Exploring the World of Insects*, and *Portraits of the Rainforest*.

ROSS GELBSPAN is a retired editor and reporter with the *Philadelphia Bulletin*, the *Washington Post*, and the *Boston Globe*. At the *Globe* he conceived and edited a series that won a Pulitzer Prize in 1984. His first major article on climate change, which appeared on the cover of the December 1995 issue of *Harper's Magazine*, was a finalist for a National Magazine Award. In 1998, he published *The Heat Is On: The Climate Crisis, The Cover-Up, The Prescription*. That same year, Gelbspan and Dr. Paul Epstein convened a group of energy company presidents, economists, and policy experts to refine a set of strategies to address the climate crisis. Those ideas formed the core of Gelbspan's next book, *Boiling Point: How Politicians, Big Oil and Coal, Journalists, and Activists Have Fueled the Climate Crisis— and What We Can Do to Avert Disaster*. Gelbspan's website (www. heatisonline.org) was called one of the best climate change Web sites by the Pacific Institute.

WAYNE GRADY, one of Canada's foremost popular science writers, has published twenty-six books, including ten books of nonfiction, ten translations from French, and six literary anthologies of Canadian short stories and nature writing. He is also a prolific writer for magazines. He has won three Science in Society awards from the Canadian Science Writers' Association. In 2004 he collaborated with David Suzuki on the bestselling *Tree: A Life Story*. His other nonfiction works include: *The Dinosaur Project*, *The Quiet Limit of the World*, *Bringing Back the Dodo: Lessons in Natural and Unnatural History*, and *The Bone Museum*. He won the Governor-General's Award for Translation for *On the Eighth Day* by Antonine Maillet, was nominated for the 2005 Governor General's Award for his translation of Francine D'Amour's *Return from Africa*, and received the John Glassco Prize for translation. He lives near Kingston, Ontario.

PAUL HAWKEN is an environmentalist, entrepreneur, journalist, and bestselling author of seven books, including *The Ecology of Commerce and Natural Capitalism*. His new book is *Blessed Unrest: How the Largest Movement in the World Came Into Being and Why No One Saw It Coming*. His books have been published in over fifty countries in twenty-seven languages and have sold over two million copies. He has dedicated his life to sustainability and changing the relationship between business and the environment, and he is head of Natural Capital Institute (www.naturalcapital.org), a nonprofit organization based in Sausalito, California.

DAVID HELVARG is President of the Blue Frontier Campaign (www.bluefront.org) and the author of *Blue Frontier: Dispatches from America's Ocean Wilderness*, *The War Against the Greens* and *50 Ways to Save the Ocean*. He is editor of the *Ocean and Coastal Conservation Guide*, organizer of several "Blue Vision" conferences for ocean activists, and winner of Coastal Living magazine's 2005 Leadership Award. Helvarg worked as a war correspondent in Northern Ireland and Central America and reported from every continent, including Antarctica. An award-winning journalist, he has produced more than forty broadcast documentaries and his work has appeared in the *New York Times*, *Smithsonian*, *Popular Science*, and the *Nation*.

DR. HEIKE K. LOTZE is an Assistant Professor in Marine Biology at Dalhousie University, Halifax, Canada, and currently holds the Canada Research Chair in Marine Renewable Resources. She has a strong interest in how human impacts alter marine species and ocean ecosystems. In her research, she tries to reconstruct the long-term history of human-induced changes in the ocean, to disentangle the cumulative effects of multiple human activities, and to analyze the consequences of human-induced changes on the structure and functioning of oceans ecosystems. Dr. Lotze received her Master's in Biology and PhD in Biological Oceanography from Kiel University in Germany. She worked as a postdoctoral fellow and research associate at Dalhousie University, the Alfred-Wegner Institute for Polar and Marine Research in Bremerhaven, Germany, and participated in several working groups at the National Center for Ecological Analysis and Synthesis in Santa Barbara, California.

JOHN LUCCHESI was born and raised in Cairo, Egypt, where his Italian family had lived for two generations. He obtained a PhD in Genetics from the University of California. Following two years of postdoctoral training in the Institute of Molecular Biology at the University of Oregon, he joined the University of North Carolina in Chapel Hill, where he became Cary C. Boshamer Professor of Biology and Genetics. In 1979 he was appointed Adjunct Professor of Genetics, Duke University; in 1983, he was named Senior Fellow of Churchill College, Cambridge University, UK. In 1990 he joined the Department of Biology at Emory University as Asa G. Candler Professor of Biology and Chair. He has served on numerous National Institutes of Health panels, including chairing the Genetics Study Section of the Division of Research Grants. He is a Fellow of the AAAS and former President of the Genetics Society of America and was Vice President of the XVII International Congress of Genetics in 1993. His research laboratory, continuously supported by the National Institute of General Medical Sciences from 1966 to date, has focused on molecular genetics.

DR. SHERILYN MACGREGOR is a lecturer in the School of Politics, International Relations and Philosophy at Keele University in the UK. She has been teaching and writing about environmental and feminist politics since the late 1990s, when she received her PhD in the Faculty of Environmental Studies at York University. She is a past editor of *Women and Environments International* magazine and she is currently an editor of *Environmental Politics* journal. Her recent book, *Beyond Mothering Earth: Ecological Citizenship and the Politics of Care*, draws on interviews with women activists in Toronto to highlight tensions between the theory and practice of green citizenship. She was born in Ottawa and now lives in the English Lake District.

RICHARD MABEY is the author of some thirty books of literary non-fiction, including *Whistling in the Dark: In Pursuit of the Nightingale, Beechcombings: the narratives of Trees*, the ground-breaking and best-selling "cultural flora" *Flora Britannica*, and *Gilbert White*, which won the Whitbread Biography Award. His recent memoir, *Nature Cure*, which describes how reconnecting with the wild helped him break free from debilitating depression, was short-listed for three major literary awards. He writes for the *Independent*, the *Guardian,* and the *Times*, and contributes frequently to BBC radio. In the 1980s he sat on the UK government's advisory body, the Nature Conservancy Council. He has been awarded honorary doctorates by St Adrews and Essex universities for his contributions to nature writing.

DOUG MOSS is founder of Earth Action Network, Inc. (EAN), based in Norwalk, Connecticut. EAN is publisher of *E—The Environmental Magazine*, the weekly e-newsletter *OurPlanet*, the Web site emagazine.com, and the nationally syndicated weekly column *EarthTalk*, which is distributed to over 1,200 newspapers and other media outlets throughout the United States and Canada.

221

DR. JIM PEACOCK was appointed Australia's Chief Scientist in 2006. He is an award-winning molecular biologist and fervent science advocate. He is a Companion of the Order of Australia, Fellow of the Australian Academy of Science, Fellow of The Royal Society of London, the Australian Academy of Technological Sciences and Engineering, a Foreign Associate of the U.S. National Academy of Sciences, and a Foreign Fellow of the Indian National Science Academy. In 2000 he was co-recipient of the inaugural Prime Minister's Science Prize. He was awarded the BHP Bicentennial Prize for the pursuit of excellence in science and technology and the Australian Academy of Science's Burnett Medal for distinguished contributions in the biological sciences. In the mid-1960s, David Suzuki and Jim Peacock were colleague researchers in the exciting field of Drosophila genetics. They had similar research interests and both had a passion for engaging young people in science and helping them understand how our world works. Peacock has since brought the excitement of science to a broad cross-section of his local communities, and especially to Australian school students.

SHELLY PEERS is Education and Public Awareness Manager at the Australian Academy of Science and Managing Director of their Primary Connections Project. Shelly was formerly Senior Project Officer to the Director of the Queensland Studies Authority. She was Manager of the Science Project for Brisbane Catholic Education from 2000 to 2003. Shelly worked on the development of the Queensland (Years 1 to 10) Science syllabus and support materials. She is a qualified biochemist and primary teacher and holds a Master of Education (Research) focusing on teacher professional learning.

CARL SAFINA is cofounder and president of Blue Ocean Institute (www.blueocean.org), an organization that inspires a closer relationship with the sea through science, art, and literature and that

222

develops conservation solutions that are compassionate to people as well as to ocean wildlife. Safina is the award-winning author of more than a hundred publications on ecology and oceans, including a new foreword to Rachel Carson's *The Sea Around Us*, and of the books *Voyage of the Turtle, Eye of the Albatross,* and *Song for the Blue Ocean.* He has honorary doctorates from SUNY and Long Island University and is Adjunct Professor at Stony Brook University. Safina is an elected member of the Explorers Club, a recipient of the Pew Scholar's Award in Conservation and the Environment, a World Wildlife Fund Senior Fellow, a recipient of Chicago's Brookfield Zoo's Rabb Medal, and winner of a MacArthur "genius" Fellowship, among other honors.

DR. MICHAEL SHERMER is Founding Publisher of *Skeptic* magazine (www.skeptic.com), Executive Director of the Skeptics Society, a columnist for *Scientific American,* host of the Skeptics Distinguished Science Lecture Series at the California Institute of Technology, and cohost and producer of the Family Channel television series *Exploring the Unknown.* He is author of *Why Darwin Matters: Evolution and the Case Against Intelligent Design, Science Friction: Where the Known Meets the Unknown, The Science of Good and Evil: Why People Cheat, Gossip, Share, Care, and Follow the Golden Rule,* and a biography, *In Darwin's Shadow,* about the co-discoverer of natural selection, Alfred Russel Wallace. He also wrote *The Borderlands of Science, Denying History, How We Believe: Science, Skepticism, and the Search for God,* and *Why People Believe Weird Things.* Dr. Shermer has been interviewed for numerous documentaries and frequently appears on news and current event programs as a skeptic of weird and extraordinary claims.

223

ALAN WEISMAN is an award-winning journalist, nonfiction writer, and radio producer. He is the author of *The World Without Us*; the memoir *An Echo In My Blood*; *Gaviotas: A Village to Reinvent the World*; and *La Frontera: The United States Border With Mexico*. His work has appeared in the *New York Times Magazine*, the *Los Angeles Times Magazine*, *Atlantic Monthly*, *Harper's*, *Mother Jones*, *Orion*, and *Audubon*, and on National Public Radio and Public Radio International. A senior radio producer for Homelands Productions, he is also Laureate Associate Professor in Journalism and Latin American Studies at the University of Arizona. He lives in western Massachusetts.

ROBYN WILLIAMS, a science journalist and broadcaster, has conducted countless interviews with scientists on Australian television programs such as *Quantum* and *Catalyst*, narrated the *Nature of Australia* series, and appeared in *World Safari* with David Attenborough. Williams has served as President of the Australian Museum Trust, Chairman of the Commission for the Future, and President of the Australian Science Communicators and was the first journalist elected as a Fellow Member of the Australian Academy of Science. He has received honorary doctorates in Science from the University of Sydney and Macquarie and Deakin universities. The ANU awarded him a Doctorate of Law, and he is Visiting Professor at the University of New South Wales and Adjunct Professor at the University of Queensland. A Reuters Fellowship at Oxford University allowed him time to write his autobiography, *And Now for Something Completely Different*. Williams has written more than ten books, the latest being a novel, *2007: A True Story, Waiting to Happen*.

DR. BORIS WORM is a marine biologist and Assistant Professor in Marine Conservation Biology in the Department of Biology, Dalhousie University in Halifax, Nova Scotia. He studied biology in Germany and Canada and received his PhD in Biological Oceanography from the University of Kiel. His research focuses on the causes and consequences of changes in marine biodiversity and its conservation on a global scale. Large predators are of particular interest to him, as they are among the most endangered marine wildlife and can play an important role in the functioning of marine ecosystems.

RONALD WRIGHT, novelist, historian, and essayist, has won prizes in all three genres and is published in more than a dozen languages. His nonfiction includes the bestseller *Stolen Continents*, winner of the Gordon Montador Award and chosen as a book of the year by the *Independent* and the *Sunday Times*; *Time Among the Maya*; and an acclaimed collection of travel pieces, *Home and Away*. His first novel, *A Scientific Romance*, won the David Higham Prize for Fiction and was deemed book of the year by the *Globe and Mail*, the *Sunday Times*, and the *New York Times*. Wright's 2004 Massey Lectures, *A Short History of Progress*, looks at the modern human predicament in light of the ten-thousand-year experiment with civilization. Wright is a frequent contributor to the *Times Literary Supplement* and has written and presented documentaries for radio and television on both sides of the Atlantic. He was born in England and educated at Cambridge and now lives in British Columbia.

225

NOTES

Notes refer to direct quotes only.

"*The Real Stuff*" BY RICHARD MABEY

(49) Lewis Thomas, *The Lives of a Cell: Notes of a Biology Watcher* (New York: Bantam Books, 1974).

"*The Ecologist*" BY PAUL HAWKEN

(66) Fritjof Capra, *The Web of Life: A New Scientific Understanding of Living Systems* (New York: Anchor, 1997), page 279.

(70) Chico Mendes, from an opening statement to secretariat of the Convention on Biological Diversity, by Ahmed Djog-hlaf, Curitba, Brazil, March 27, 2006.

(72) Martin Luther King, Jr., "Beyond Vietnam," address delivered to the Clergy and Laymen concerned about Vietnam, at Riverside Church, New York City, April 4, 1967

(75) David James Duncan, *God Laughs and Plays: Churchless Sermons in Response to the Preachments of the Fundamentalist Right* (Triad Books, 2007), page 118.

"*Three Ships*" BY SHERILYN MACGREGOR

(78) Monique Wittig, *The Straight Mind and Other Essays.* (London: Harvester Wheatsheaf, 1992), p. 13.

(79) Virginia Woolf, "Professions for Women," in *Three Guineas,* ed. N. Black. (Oxford: Blackwell Publishers, 2001).

(81) Vandana Shiva, "Women and Religion in the context of globalization," in *Women and Religion in a Globalized World: A Conversation of Women's and Religious Leaders,* convened by the Peace Council and the Centre for Health and Social Policy, Chiang Mai, Thailand, p. 64. Available at http://www.chsp.org/Women_

and_Religion_in_a_Globalized_World.pdf.

(87) Virginia Woolf quoted in Naomi Black's introduction to
Three Guineas, ed. N. Black. (Oxford: Blackwell Publishers,
2001), p. xxxv.

"The Mechanical Savior: Nature and the Illusion of Technology"
BY WAYNE GRADY

(99) Both Bush and Harper were widely quoted in the newspapers
in the fall of 2005 (Bush) and 2006 (Harper). See, for example,
the *Toronto Globe and Mail* for October 14, 2006: "Mr. Harper said
yesterday that technological improvements will ultimately reduce
total [carbon dioxide] emissions over the long term." Both leaders
have since reiterated their faith in technology. See, for example,
Harper's extolling of the seques-tering of carbon dioxide in Alberta
and Bush's recent equation of technology with "innovation" and
the entrepreneurial spirit: www.whitehouse.gov/infocus/technology.

(99) David F. Noble, in *The Religion of Technology: The Divinity of Man
and the Spirit of Invention* (New York: Alfred A. Knopf, 1997),
discusses the history of technology and its close links with the
Church at the end of the Dark Ages. He goes on to examine faith-
based technologies as they pertain to atomic weaponry, space
exploration, artificial intelligence, and genetic engineering,
which is expected to restore humanity to Eden and create
"the New Adam."

(101) Included in C.P. Snow, *The Two Cultures* (Cambridge: Cambridge
University Press, 1993).

(102) *Shirley* was published in 1849 under the pseudonym Currer Bell,
when Charlotte was thirty-three.

(102) Delivered on February 7, 1812, three years after Byron took his
seat in the House.

(103) All quotes from *Erewhon* are from the Penguin edition of 1974,
pp. 199, 6, 207, and 206.

(104) All quotes from "Findings," the final page of *Harper's* magazine,
various issues throughout 2006 and 2007, which reports without
comment recent innovations in technology.

(105) John A. Livingstone, *Rogue Primate: An Exploration of Human
Domestication* (Toronto: Key Porter Books, 1994), p. 13.

(105) Sigmund Freud, *Civilization and Its Discontents*, first published in 1930 as *Des Unbehagen in der Kultur*. My quotes from the Penguin edition, translated in 2002 and republished in 2004, pp. 34, 36, 42, and 44.

(108) Thomas Powers, writing in the *New York Review of Books* (September 22, 2005, page 75) in a review of books about J.R. Oppenheimer, notes that "when I first started to talk to Los Alamos scientists about the invention of nuclear weapons twenty years ago, I assumed that they had long since confronted and sorted out the rights and wrongs of the case, but I soon found that it wasn't so. At an early date their thinking had frozen around a handful of simple ideas—building the bomb was justified because the Germans were trying to do it . . ."

(108) Personal communication.

(109) Friedrich Georg Juenger, *The Failure of Technology: Perfection Without Purpose*, completed in 1939 but not published in German (as *Illusionen der Technik*) until 1946, and translated into English in 1949. Pages 20–24 passim.

"Toward a Real Kyoto Protocol" BY ROSS GELBSPAN

(128) Jim Hansen, "Greenland ice cap breaking up at twice the rate it was five years ago, says scientist Bush tried to gag," *The Independent* (UK), Feb. 17, 2006.

"Fools' Paradise" BY RONALD WRIGHT

(160) William Camden quoted in *The Idea of Prehistory* by Glyn Daniel (London: Pelican, 1962) pp. 14–15.

(161) Letter of Francisco de Toledo, March 25, 1571, quoted in *Saqsaywaman 1* (July 1970), ed. Luis Pardo, p. 144.

(161) Jacob Roggeveen, quoted in *Easter Island, Earth Island* by Paul Bahn and John Flenley (London: Thames & Hudson, 1992), p. 13.

(162) Captain James Cook, quoted in *Easter Island* by Catherine and Michel Orliac, trans. Paul Bahn (New York: Abrams, 1995), p. 17.

(167) Paul Bahn and John Flenley, *Easter Island, Earth Island* (London: Thames & Hudson, 1992), pp. 213, 218.

"The Geography of Hope" BY THOMAS BERGER

(196) Wallace Stegner, "Wilderness Idea," in *The Sound of Mountain Water* (Garden City, NJ: Doubleday, 1969).

ACKNOWLEDGMENTS

Quotes at the beginning of each section are all from
The David Suzuki Reader (Vancouver: Greystone Books, 2003).

"The Old Man On His Back" by Sharon Butala appeared in a
different form in *The Structurist,* edited by Dr. Eli Bornstein,
issue 43/44 (2003–2004).

"The Real Stuff" by Richard Mabey is adapted from an article in
Granta 93, 2006.

"My Credo" by Helen Caldicott is adapted from an article in
The Independent, November 12, 2006.

"The Ecologist" by Paul Hawken appeared in another form in *Blessed Unrest:
How the Largest Movement in the World Came Into Being and Why No One Saw It
Coming* (New York: Viking/Penguin, 2001).

"Why We Should Care About the Ocean" by Heike K. Lotze and Boris Worm
was inspired by the "Linking marine biodiversity and ecosystem services"
Working Group supported by the National Center for Ecological Analysis and
Synthesis, which is funded by the National Science Foundation, the University
of California, and the University of California–Santa Barbara. The authors
thank E. Barbier, N. Beaumont, J.E. Duffy, C. Folke, B. Halpern, J. Jackson, F.
Micheli, S. Palumbi, E. Sala. K. Selkoe, J. Stachowicz, and R. Watson for their
thoughts and discussions, and N. Baron, N. Loder, and I. Milewski for asking
the right questions. They are also deeply grateful to the late R.A. Myers for his
inspiration and support and his great passion for the ocean and for science.

"Fools' Paradise" by Ronald Wright is adapted from *A Short History of Progress* by Ronald Wright (Toronto: House of Anansi, 2004) and was published in slightly different form in the *Times Literary Supplement*, November 19, 2004.

"The Geography of Hope" by Thomas Berger is adapted from an article that appeared in the *Globe and Mail*, September 2005.